GUITAR *signature licks*

JAZZ GUITAR

ISBN 0-634-02266-0

HAL•LEONARD®
CORPORATION

7777 W. BLUEMOUND RD. P.O. BOX 13819 MILWAUKEE, WI 53213

Visit Hal Leonard Online at
www.halleonard.com

CONTENTS

PAGE	TITLE	ARTIST	CD TRACK
3	Preface		
4	A Jazz Guitar Axology		
6	The Recording		
6	Discography		1
			2
8	ST. THOMAS	Jim Hall	3
15		Tal Farlow	4
21		Kenny Burrell	5
27	ALL BLUES	George Benson	6
35		Kenny Burrell	7
39		Pat Martino	8
42	SO WHAT	Barney Kessel	9
47		George Benson	10-11
57	ALL THE THINGS YOU ARE	Hank Garland	12
63		Pat Metheny	13
71	HONEYSUCKLE ROSE	Joe Pass and Herb Ellis	14
76		Charlie Christian	15
79	SATIN DOLL	Howard Roberts	16
86		Joe Pass	17
92	YESTERDAYS	Johnny Smith	18
95		Tal Farlow	19
102		Wes Montgomery	20
108	MISTY	Barney Kessel	21
111		Wes Montgomery	22
121		Howard Roberts	23
128	I'LL REMEMBER APRIL	Johnny Smith	24
133		Grant Green	25
142	HOW INSENSITIVE	Pat Martino	26
151		Emily Remler	27
158	Guitar Notation Legend		

PREFACE

This volume is a first. It presents ten of the most frequently played and important tunes from the mainstream jazz genre in the signature licks format. You'll find the favorite compositions of Miles Davis, Sonny Rollins, and Duke Ellington alongside perennial standards from Jerome Kern, Erroll Garner, and Antonio Carlos Jobim interpreted by the leading exponents of jazz guitar.

Every effort has been made to locate renditions of the material which contain definitive performances by the individual artists and which provide significant contrasting approaches between the various players. Accordingly, a wide selection of tunes in varied settings from duets and trios to larger ensembles is offered. There is something from every major epoch. The pieces range from the genesis of jazz guitar in the swing style of Charlie Christian to the subsequent innovations of Kenny Burrell, Tal Farlow, Jim Hall, and Barney Kessel, and the hard bop and mainstream tangents of Wes Montgomery, Joe Pass, George Benson, and Pat Martino.

In understanding the way in which a jazz artist approaches the core repertoire, one can glean much about the creative process at work and still more about the unique attributes of an individual and the choices an improvising musician makes during performance. That is the essence of this volume—to present not only the actual notes played (via the note-for-note transcriptions), but to explore the paths taken by the player during the heat of the moment. Annotations provide technical analysis and performance notes shed light on the musical idiosyncrasies of each excerpt while biographical sketches underscore the historical significance of each guitarist. Finally, the authentic matching audio with backing tracks will facilitate the acquisition of your own powers of improvisation. Through studying and assimilating the vocabulary and the work of the masters, you will be on your way to finding and developing your own voice and saying with it what cannot be expressed with words—the goal of improvising musicians everywhere.

Enjoy.

Wolf Marshall

A JAZZ GUITAR AXOLOGY

(All instruments from the collection of the author. Photos by Robb Lawrence)

The earliest jazz guitars were archtop acoustics. These were fitted with electronics that still exist to this day in either of two configurations: with built-in pickups or with floating pickups. Pictured above and illustrative of the two are an ES-175 with the famous "Charlie Christian" bar pickup and a 1940 Gibson L-5 with a floating DeArmond Rhythm Chief system. Notable players of the bar pickup include Charlie Christian, Oscar Moore, Tal Farlow, Jimmy Raney, Barney Kessel, Hank Garland, and bluesman T-Bone Walker. Players who have used floating pickups include Kenny Burrell, George Benson, Johnny Smith, and Pat Martino. In the background is a mint-condition 1952 Gibson GA-75 with a 15-inch Jensen speaker—the top-of-the-line of the GA amp series. The GA models were the paragon of 1950s jazz tone and associated with numerous jazz guitarists such as Tal Farlow, Howard Roberts, Barney Kessel, and Jim Hall.

Arch-top electric guitars appeared with single-coil pickups in the late 1940s and were popular throughout the 1950s during the heyday of bebop. Humbucking pickups on arch-top electrics became the norm for jazz guitars after 1958. Shown on the bottom of the previous page are two incarnations of the workhorse jazz box, the Gibson ES-175, with P-90s (left), and humbuckers (right). Jim Hall, Herb Ellis, and Grant Green are among the most well-known P-90 jazz players. Guitarists who have favored humbuckers include Wes Montgomery, Joe Pass, Pat Martino, Pat Metheny, and Emily Remler. In the background are two classic Fender combo amplifiers used by countless jazz guitarists: the blackface Deluxe Reverb (right) and the ever-popular blackface Twin Reverb (left).

Pictured here is one of the most important jazz guitars in history: Howard Robert's highly modified archtop electric known as "The Black Guitar." Previously owned by Herb Ellis, it began as a late-1930s ES-150. HR changed its body shape (into a thinner two-inch depth with a unique double cutaway), fingerboard and neck (ebony with dot inlays on a 25 1/4-inch scale), electronics (P-90 pickup), and finish (black). This was the first "jazz guitar" I ever heard on record as a kid on the album *H.R. Is A Dirty Guitar Player*. Coincidentally, I purchased this extraordinary instrument from Howard's wife, Patty. The pleasantly fortuitous result is that you will be able to hear his music played on his guitar again on the signature licks track of "Satin Doll." In the background is the contemporary standard for jazz guitar amplification, the Polytone Mini-Brute II. Polytone amps are used by Joe Pass, George Benson, Herb Ellis, and is currently employed by Jim Hall, Howard Alden, and Jimmy Bruno.

THE RECORDING

Wolf Marshall: guitar
Mike Sandberg: drums & percussion
Dennis Croy: bass
Fred Kaplan: piano & organ
John Nau: piano and organ on "Yesterdays" and "Misty" (Wes Montgomery versions)
Barry Gurton: vibes
Roland Coltrane: tenor sax

Special thanks to Brian Vance of Gibson USA for my beautiful workhorse, the Gibson ES-175DN, heard on many of these tracks, and to Del Breckenfeld and Alex Perez of Fender Musical Instruments for the '65 Twin-Reverb amp used throughout this recording.

Extra special thanks to Reed Kotler for his marvelous TR-1000 Digital Music Study Recorder which enabled me to take down the nuances and intricacies of these performances and bring them to you as transcriptions.

I will be forever grateful to Pat Martino, Johnny Smith, Bobby Rose, Hank and Billy Garland, Roger Borys, Kenny Burrell, Sid Jacobs, Howard Alden, and Henry Johnson who took time from their busy schedules to share historical data and guitar insights with me during the writing of this volume.

For more on jazz guitar and the music of the artists contained in this volume, please visit *Wolf Marshalls Guitarland* at wolfmarshall.com on the worldwide web.

DISCOGRAPHY

The titles in this volume came from the following recordings:

1. *ALONE TOGETHER,* Jim Hall/Ron Carter Duo. (Milestone OJCCD-467-2)
   "St.Thomas"

2. *CHROMATIC PALETTE,* Tal Farlow. (Concord Jazz CCD-4154)
   "St. Thomas"

3. *LAID BACK,* Kenny Burrell. (32 Jazz 32064)
   "St.Thomas", "All Blues"

4. *GEORGE BENSON LIVE (THE EARLY YEARS),* George Benson. (GWP 9907).
   "All Blues"

5. *INTRODUCING ERIC KLOSS,* Eric Kloss. (Prestige 7442)
   "All Blues" (Pat Martino version)

6. *MOONLIGHT IN VERMONT,* Johnny Smith Quintet. (Roulette CDP 7977472)
   "Yesterdays," "I'll Remember April"

7. *TAL FARLOW,* Tal Farlow. (Verve Jazz Masters 41: 314 527 365-2)
   "Yesterdays"

8. *WES MONTGOMERY TRIO,* Wes Montgomery. (Riverside OJCCD-034-2)
   "Yesterdays"

9. *JAZZ WINDS FROM A NEW DIRECTION,* Hank Garland. (Sony Music WK 75027)
   "All The Things You Are"

10. *QUESTION AND ANSWER,* Pat Metheny. (Geffen 9 24293-2)
    "All The Things You Are"

11. *THE POLLWINNERS EXPLORING THE SCENE,* Barney Kessel, Shelly Manne, &
    Ray Brown. (Contemporary OJCD-969-2)
    "So What," "Misty"

12. *BEYOND THE BLUE HORIZON,* George Benson. (CTI ZK 65130)
    "So What"

13. *JAZZ CONCORD,* Herb Ellis & Joe Pass. (Concord CCD2-4788-2)
    "Honeysuckle Rose"

14. *CHARLIE CHRISTIAN,* Charlie Christian. (The Best of Jazz: The Swing Era 4032)
    "Honeysuckle Rose"

15. *DIRTY N FUNKY,* Howard Roberts Quartet. (EMI-Capitol 72438-19483-2-3)
    "Satin Doll"

16. *PORTRAITS OF DUKE ELLINGTON,* Joe Pass. (Pablo PACD-2310-716-2)
    "Satin Doll"

17. *IMPRESSIONS: THE VERVE JAZZ SIDES,* Wes Montgomery. (Verve 314 521 690-2)
    "Misty"

18. *ALL-TIME GREAT INSTRUMENTAL HITS,* Howard Roberts Quartet. (Capitol ST 2609)
    "Misty"

19. *STANDARDS,* Grant Green. (Blue Note CDP 7243 8 21284 2 7)
    "I'll Remember April"

20. *FOOTPRINTS,* Pat Martino. (32 Jazz 32021)
    "How Insensitive"

21. *RETROSPECTIVE VOLUME ONE,* Emily Remler. (Concord Jazz CCD-4453)
    "How Insensitive"

Of inestimable value and enthusiastically recommended are the live performances featuring
most of the aforementioned jazz guitarists contained on the following videos:

1. *LEGENDS OF JAZZ GUITAR: VOLUMES 1, 2, and 3* —Vestapol 13009, Vestapol
   13033, and Vestapol 13043.

2. *THE GENIUS OF JOE PASS* —Vestapol 13073

3. *JOE PASS IN CONCERT* —Vestapol 13025

4. *WES MONTGOMERY 1965—BELGIUM*—Vestapol 13084

All selections transcribed by Wolf Marshall

ST. THOMAS
By Sonny Rollins

Tenor saxophonist Sonny Rollins penned one of the greatest and most enduring jazz classics with his calypso-based line "St. Thomas." Originally recorded on the *Saxophone Colossus* album (1956), "St. Thomas" is a simple 32-bar tune in ABAB form distinguished by a catchy 16-measure theme. A perennial favorite among jam tunes, "St. Thomas" is a must-know piece in the genre, and here affords us three distinctly different approaches from Jim Hall, Tal Farlow, and Kenny Burrell.

Jim Hall

Fig. 1 — Head and Solo

Jim Hall was one of the first post-Charlie Christian guitarists to offer a truly different concept of the instrument. Born in Buffalo, NY, Hall was raised in the Cleveland area and graduated from the Cleveland Institute of Music where he majored in music theory and pursued classical composition. He joined the Los Angeles jazz scene in 1955 and gained public attention through his work with the Chico Hamilton Quintet and the Jimmy Giuffre Trio. In 1958, Hall moved to New York City and began working with Sonny Rollins, ultimately playing on Rollins's 1962 masterpiece *The Bridge.* He is also well-known for his contributions to the music of Paul Desmond, John Lewis, Eric Dolphy, Ornette Coleman, and his partnerships with Bill Evans and Ron Carter.

The definitive jazz-guitar rendition of "St. Thomas" comes from the Jim Hall-Ron Carter *Alone Together* set. It is appropriate to look at Hall's version first, not only because of his connection with Sonny Rollins but also because he has taken the Rollins-inspired notion of thematic development in jazz to sublime heights; this is abundantly self-evident in his melodious and well-textured reading of "St. Thomas." Pat Metheny cites Hall as "the greatest living guitarist," and who are we to disagree? Instead, let "St. Thomas" argue the case musically in his favor.

Personnel:	Duet. Jim Hall, guitar; Ron Carter, bass.
Recorded:	August 4,1972, at The Playboy Club, New York City.
Arrangement:	The Hall-Carter rendition is in the standard key of C and taken at medium tempo. The essence of the arrangement is in its interplay. This is an intuitive and sensitive jazz duet captured spontaneously before a sympathetic audience. Hall begins with a solo statement of the opening phrase and Carter answers in the fourth measure. This lays the ground for the tune's contrapuntal treatment. Hall states the head succinctly and elegantly in single notes and octaves. It is played twice, the second time B with variations, before the solo commences in C . Hall takes six choruses, C through H , each building in complexity and intensity.
Signatures:	Hall's solo is an illustrative example of his compositional approach and use of *thematic development* in improvisation. Each chorus contains a theme or central idea which is elaborated texturally, harmonically, and rhythmically, and is pursued to a logical conclusion. Noteworthy is Hall's application of varied tex-

tures: single notes, octaves, small two- and three-part chords, and larger five-note chords all moving progressively toward a climax in the final chorus.

Performance notes: "St. Thomas" contains a brilliant mix of guitar textures, colors and articulations. The slurred octaves in the head (measures 9–12 and 25–28) are plucked with the fingers. The second statement of the head [B] is played with *palm muting* for an ear-catching percussive effect. Hall's solo is predominately chordal and rhythmic. It begins sparsely in [C] with a pedal-tone episode exploiting the open G string for a *drone effect*. In [D], the drone effect is emphasized by longer duration, greater frequency, and the use of dyads. In [E], Hall develops mixed textures: three-note chords interpolated with octaves. Two specific three-note voicings introduced in measures 65-66 lay the groundwork for most of what follows. These shapes are comprised of an octave with an inner tone a 6th above the lowest note (for example: C major voiced as either E–C–E or G–E–G). The simplicity and malleability of this chord allows for many applications, and Hall demonstrates this in [E] through [H] where the same forms are used in a variety of harmonic situations. George Benson also makes great use of this chord type in his style. In [E], Hall develops a pattern of rhythmically-charged octave figures which acts as a "turnaround" in the final four measures. This becomes thematic and is repeated in the ensuing choruses.

Sound: Jim Hall has always boasted one of jazz guitar's richest tones. His signature sound emanated from the combination of a Gibson ES-175 with a single P-90 pickup (previously owned by Howard Roberts) and an early 1950s Gibson GA-50 combo amp. He uses medium picks and light-gauge flat-wound strings.

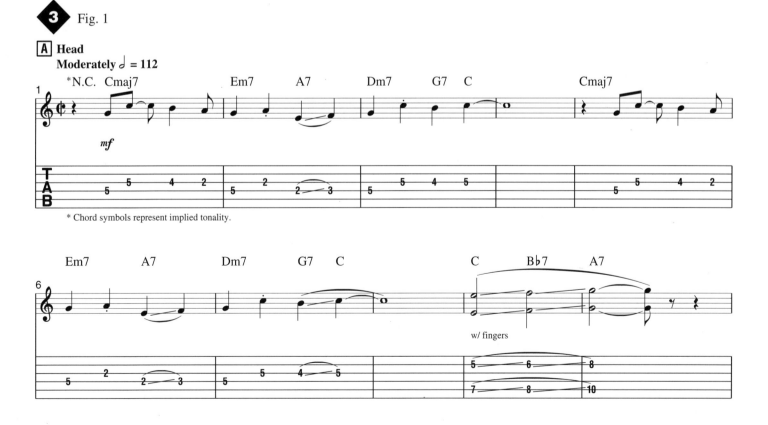

3 ▶ Fig. 1

[A] **Head**
Moderately ♩ = 112

*N.C. Cmaj7   Em7   A7   Dm7   G7   C   Cmaj7

mf

* Chord symbols represent implied tonality.

Em7   A7   Dm7   G7   C   C   B♭7   A7

w/ fingers

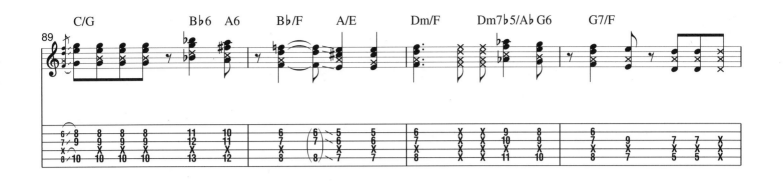

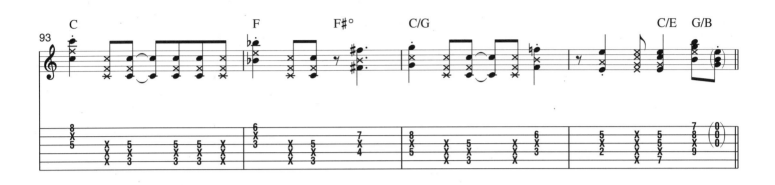

G Fifth Chorus

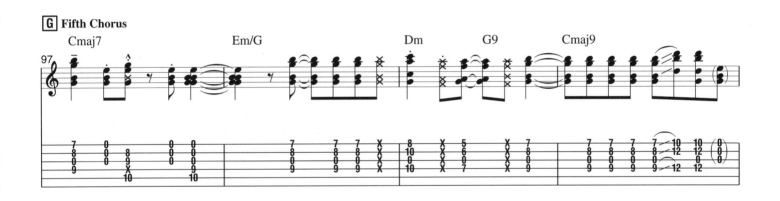

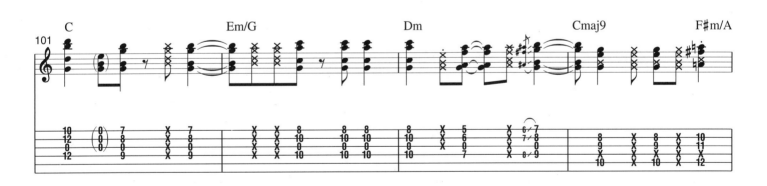

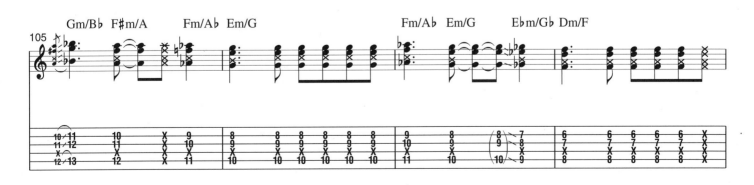

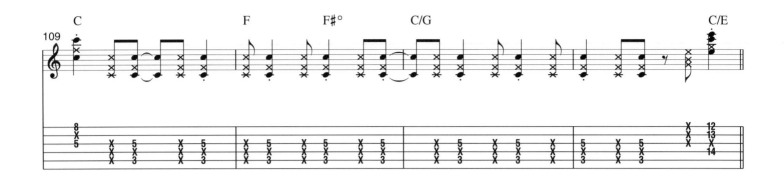

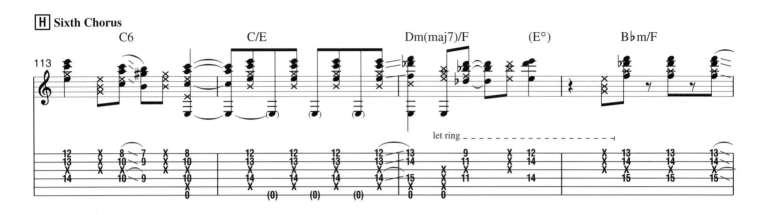

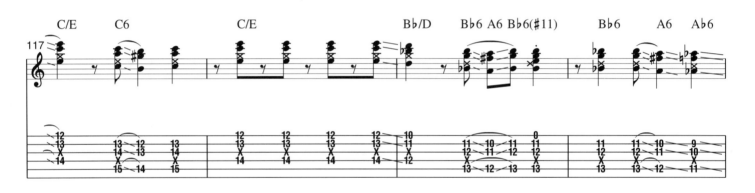

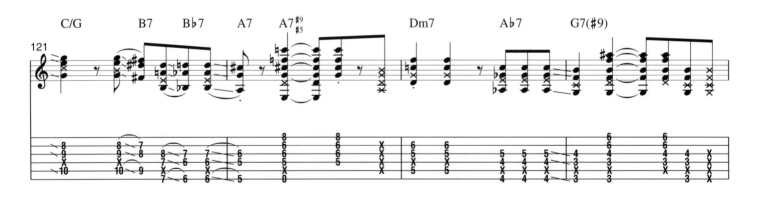

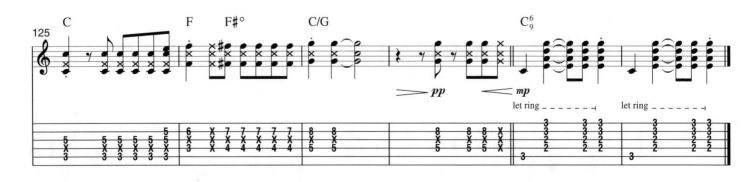

Tal Farlow

Fig. 2 — Head and Solo

Tal Farlow, the virtuoso of 1950s jazz guitar, was a late bloomer who didn't pick up the instrument until he was in his 20s. A self-taught player, Farlow was originally inspired by Charlie Christian and subsequently made his name with Buddy DeFranco, Artie Shaw, and the Red Norvo Trio. His brilliant bop-oriented passagework was the guiding light for a slew of guitarists who came of age in the 1950s including Pat Martino and John McLaughlin. Farlow harbored a distaste for the music business which resulted in unpredictable periods of absence from the public eye after 1958. He resurfaced at jazz festivals and with irregular guest appearances by the late 1960s, and began recording again as a leader for Concord in 1976. Farlow passed away in 1998, leaving a legacy as large as his gigantic hands and a musical catalog which continues to inspire.

Tal Farlow tackled "St. Thomas" on his 1981 *Chromatic Palette* record, providing a look at his later style. By contrast with Hall's tight thematic treatment, Farlow interprets "St. Thomas" as a straight-ahead blowing piece. His version is a showcase for his formidable technique and adventurous harmonic approach; it reflects a well-known penchant for long phrases of fleet single-note lines, faster tempos, and a sharper, more aggressive attack.

Personnel:	Trio. Tal Farlow, guitar; Tommy Flanagan, piano; Gary Mazzaroppi, bass.
Recorded:	January, 1981, at Soundmixers, New York City.
Arrangement:	Farlow's version is also in the standard key of C. The drummerless guitar-piano-bass trio is a format Farlow frequently exploited in his career. The head is a straight reading of the melody in A and B. Farlow then takes five improvised solo choruses in C, D, E, F, and G.
Signatures:	The long strings of single-note lines found throughout this solo are unmistakable Tal Farlow signatures. Farlow, with his fine technique and keen harmonic sense, was one of the earliest guitarists to play long complex lines of this type. His most telling melodies embody a mixture of Charlie Christian swing melodies and bebop horn phrases, and occur in measures 41–45, 51–56, 70–77, 86–92, and 104–111. Farlow's bop lines are complemented by groove riffs in measures 33–37, 64–68, and 96–98, and an occasional vintage swing/blues lick; the latter is no doubt a vestige of his Charlie Christian influence.
Performance notes:	Tal Farlow was nicknamed the "octopus" for his large hands and extended physical reach. Farlow incorporated this uncanny technical ability as an integral part of his style and several phrases in this solo reflect this attribute. Most are found as unusual position shifts and wide stretches in the midst of eighth-note lines. Others attain greater importance as thematic lines. A particular phrase first heard at D measures 53–54 recurs in E measures 71–72 and F measures 88–89. It is comprised of three distinct elements: a diminished arpeggio (C–E♭–G♭–E♭) followed by a descending blues melody (C–G–G♭–F), and a familiar bebop figure (F–D–D♯–E).

Sound: Compared with Jim Hall's buttery tone, Farlow's sound is brighter and more penetrating. During this period, he used a 1962 Gibson prototype Tal Farlow model with two humbucking pickups. Farlow strung his guitar with medium-gauge strings and employed heavy picks. His amplifier of choice was an old Fender Twin.

4 ▸ Fig. 2

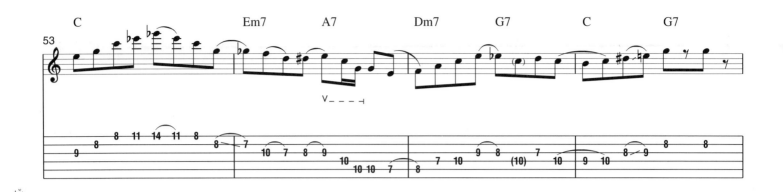

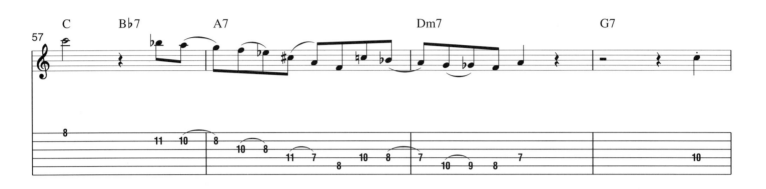

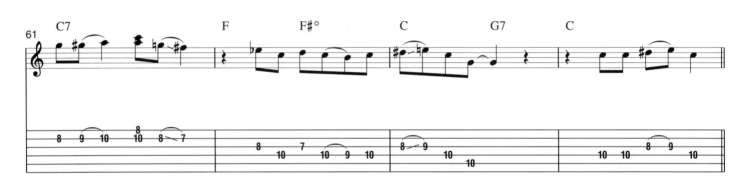

E Third Chorus

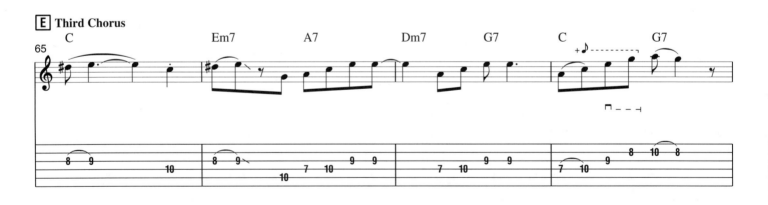

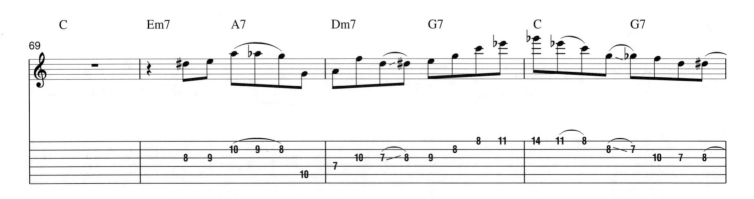

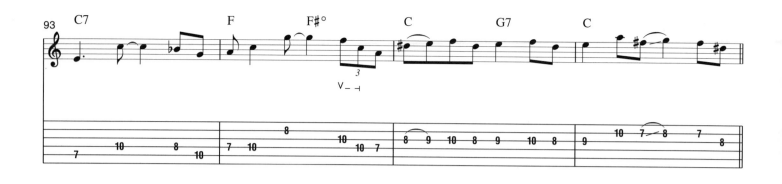

G **Fifth Chorus**

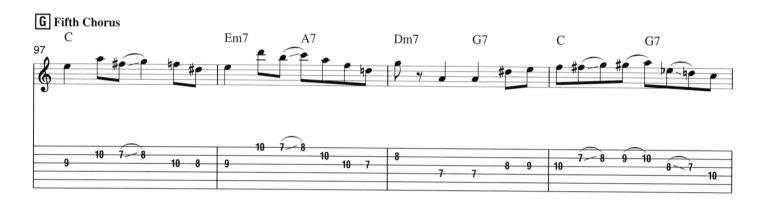

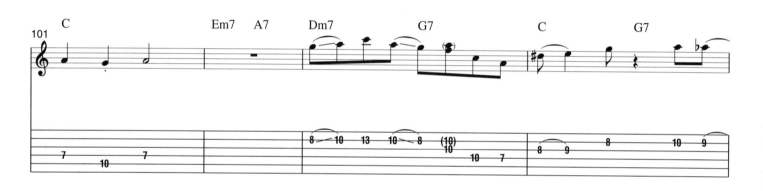

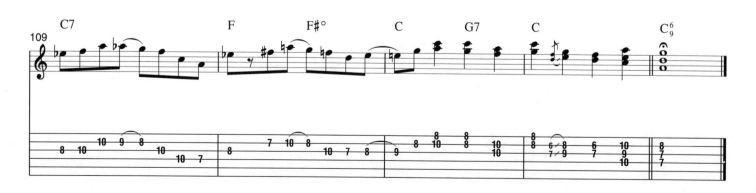

Kenny Burrell

Fig. 3 — Intro, Head, and Solo

Kenny Burrell is one of the most influential and important jazz guitarists of the post-Charlie Christian era. His broad music palette incorporates a number of playing styles including swing, bebop, funky blues, gospel, Latin, and third-stream classically-influenced jazz. Born and raised in Detroit, Burrell was originally drawn to the saxophone and was inspired to pick up the guitar after hearing Charlie Christian's horn-like swing lines. He pursued music from that point on, ultimately earning a BA in music composition from Wayne State University. His professional life began in 1951. Since then, he has racked up credits that read like a who's who in jazz. Burrell has performed with Duke Ellington, Billie Holiday, John Coltrane, Dizzy Gillespie, Benny Goodman, Oscar Peterson, Jimmy Smith, Gil Evans, Coleman Hawkins, Sonny Rollins, Stan Getz, Milt Jackson, and many others. He was an early influence on Wes Montgomery and Grant Green, and has also been hailed as inspirational by rock and blues players like Steve Howe, Robbie Krieger, and Stevie Ray Vaughan. In addition to his active performing career, he is also a professor at UCLA where he teaches a course in "Ellingtonia."

A true master of improvised music, Kenny Burrell recorded "St. Thomas" in a live club setting accompanied by bassist Rufus Reid. Their rendition is of the same intuitive caliber as the earlier Hall/Carter duo setting with some intriguing twists. The track was originally released on the *A La Carte* album and stands as one of Burrell's finest moments of his later period.

Personnel: Duet. Kenny Burrell, guitar; Rufus Reid, bass.

Recorded: August 23, 1983, at the Village West, New York City.

Arrangement: Burrell's arrangement of "St. Thomas" offers several contrasts to previous versions. He plays it in the key of G at a moderate tempo, slightly faster than Hall's but not as brisk as Farlow's, and uses an acoustic guitar for a different timbre. Moreover, he infuses the tune with a pronounced blues feeling, apparent throughout the improvisations and the 16-bar intro [A]. In Burrell's arrangement, the head [B] is played only once before his five solo choruses in [C] through [G].

Signatures: Blues inflections, typical of Burrell's style, are evident and abundant from the tune's opening melody. An obvious reference in single notes to a familiar blues turnaround is heard in measures 5–8 and 13–16. Burrell mixes textures in the head [B], employing single notes, octaves, and four-note seventh chords. The voicings and reharmonization in measures 25–30 are characteristic of his harmonic approach. In his improvisations, Burrell alternates between call-and-response riff-type melodies, blues flurries, and longer phrases in eighth-note groupings. His lines are often rhythmically based as in 33–37, 65–70, 81–86, and particularly 97–100.

Performance notes: Burrell's solo, consisting predominately of single notes, juxtaposes blues licks and diatonic melody. His diatonic melodies outline chord changes, as found in measures 81–88 and 89–91, or provide strong sequential phrases, heard in measures 42–44, 57–60, and 105–108. Typically, Burrell's blues lines employ the G blues scale (G–B♭–C–D♭–D–F) or the G minor pentatonic scale (G–B♭–C–D–F). Note the purposeful use of an ascending chromatic blues cliché in measures 47 and 64 as a cadential figure and as a component of a longer rising cadence line in 95.

Burrell's episode in measures 97–100 is a climax in the solo. It is highly rhythmic and exploits unison intervals played in a *cross-rhythm* or *hemiola* (three against four) phrasing. Here the accents clearly distinguish the three-note groups. Burrell plays off the theme in measures 105–108 to rejoin the final cadence in 109–111. Throughout his improvisations, Burrell varies his picking attack greatly. This produces a wide range of phrasing options and dynamics, from legato to staccato with sharp accents or a soft feathery touch.

Sound: For this performance, Burrell played a steel-string flat-top acoustic guitar. This is atypical, as most jazz guitarists would choose either an arch-top or a nylon-string acoustic (Burrell also played those). As such, Burrell is one of a very small handful of guitarists, and arguably the most conspicuous, to effectively exploit the sound of the flat-top acoustic in mainstream jazz.

5 ▷ Fig. 3

* Chords implied.

* Lift off slightly to mute w/ fingertip.

ALL BLUES

By Miles Davis

Trumpeter Miles Davis is one the great paternal figures of modern jazz. His *Kind Of Blue* album of 1959 redefined the music and yielded several watershed tunes. Prime among them is "All Blues," one of the most recognizable riff-based compositions in the repertory. A 12-bar blues in 6/8 meter, "All Blues" has become a jazz standard played by countless musicians. It yields a valuable study examining the contrasting approaches of George Benson, Kenny Burrell, and Pat Martino.

George Benson

Fig. 4 — Intro, Head, and Solo

George Benson enjoys a phenomenal career in music. Successful as both a jazz artist and pop star, he is fluent with the most intricate bebop music, is a soulful blues and funk player, and also excels at commercial entertainment. Born and bred in Pittsburgh, PA, Benson began recording at age 10, singing R&B singles for a local company while working as a street musician. After hearing saxophonist Charlie Parker, he was inspired to take up jazz and relocated to New York City in 1963. There he became immersed in the organ-led scene, performed with Jimmy Smith and "Brother" Jack McDuff, and cultivated a lasting friendship with mentor Wes Montgomery. Benson was "discovered" in the mid-1960s by John Hammond (who also discovered Charlie Christian, Bob Dylan, and Stevie Ray Vaughan), and subsequently forged a powerful musical presence through his work on the Columbia, Verve, A&M, and CTI labels. Benson's commercial breakthrough occurred in 1976 with the release of the *Breezin'* album and a new contract with Warner Brothers. The rest is history.

George Benson recorded "All Blues" during a live club date in 1973. His take on the tune epitomizes the atmosphere of a spontaneous Sunday afternoon jam session. The approach is casual, with Benson setting the tone from his first statement of the riff. The tune and solos grow organically from there, starting sparsely and building in dynamics, complexity, and density with each ensuing chorus.

Personnel:	Quartet. George Benson, guitar; Mickey Tucker, piano; George Duvivier, bass; Al Harewood, drums.
Recorded:	April 1973, at The Casa Caribe, Plainfield, New Jersey.
Arrangement:	Benson plays "All Blues" at a moderate tempo in the standard key of G. His arrangement is straightforward: a statement of the riff and the head followed by improvised solos. He starts the intro A unaccompanied with the two-bar core riff. The band enters in the third measure. The head is played twice in B and C, the second time with greater embellishment. In this excerpt, four of Benson's solo choruses are presented in D, E, F, and G.
Signatures:	Benson's playing is solidly blues-based, often colored with distinctively funky R&B phrasing. His bebop sensibilities complement the earthy blues quality and, in conjunction, produce a satisfying balance of approaches—a strong identifier of his style. The three-note chord forms used to play part of the melody in measures 11–12 and 23–24 are fixtures of Benson's playing. (See Hall's use of similar voicings in "St. Thomas.") Benson's

first four solo choruses feature predominantly single notes. Each progressively exposes and develops a new idea: use of space and small fragmentary motives in D, greater melodic complexity and chromaticism in E, intervallic playing, double-timed bebop lines in long 32nd-note strings and blues licks in F, and the development of quirky reverse-mordent riffs in G. Benson's penchant for wider intervals in his lines is apparent in measures 43, 52, 54–55, and 56–58.

Performance notes: Benson is equally adept at playing with plectrum or his thumb and fingers. The tone of this track indicates Benson was primarily employing his thumb to pick notes and strum chords. This is a technique he often uses for a richer, thicker sound, and one which is closely associated with Wes Montgomery. Additionally, Benson uses his thumb and fingers to pluck chords in measures 11–12 and 23–24, and to arpeggiate melodies and broken intervallic lines in 52, 54–55, and 57–58. Benson is a *linear* player who favors a slippery *horizontal approach* (up and down the length of the fingerboard), especially in his long single-note passages. These phrases frequently involve rapid and seamless position changes as evident in measures 46–49, 60–62, and 63–67. One essential point: Benson almost exclusively uses his index, middle, and ring fret-hand fingers for single-note playing. The pinky is rarely used and is generally saved for quick stretches to high notes.

Sound: Benson played a number of guitars at this point in his career. These were archtops, usually equipped with a single floating pickup (DeArmond or Johnny Smith type), and included a Gibson Johnny Smith model, a Guild Artist Award, and a D'Angelico New Yorker. His amp of choice was a Fender Twin Reverb, though he later used Polytones.

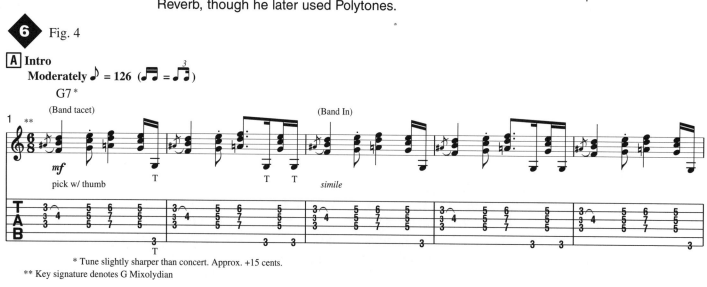

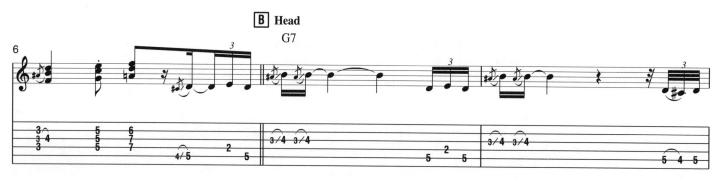

* Tremolo w/ fingerpicking.

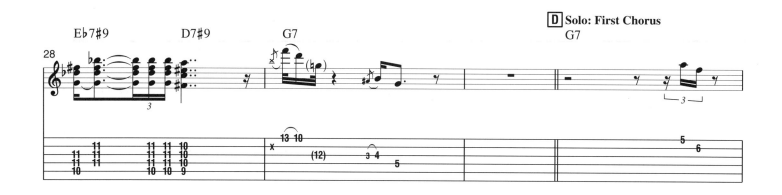

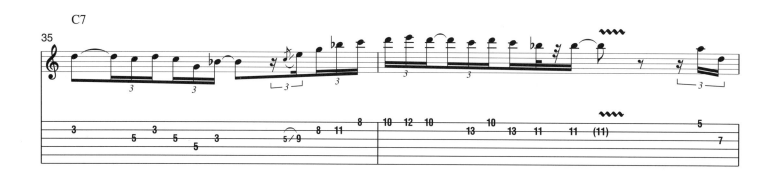

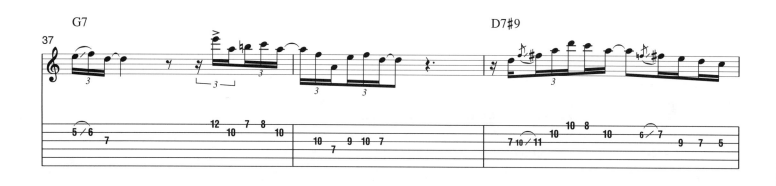

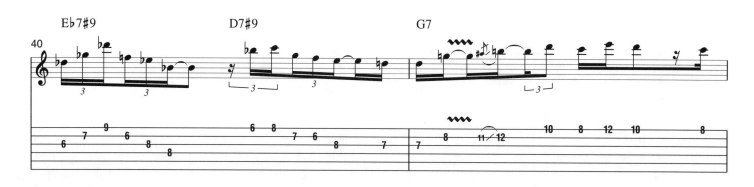

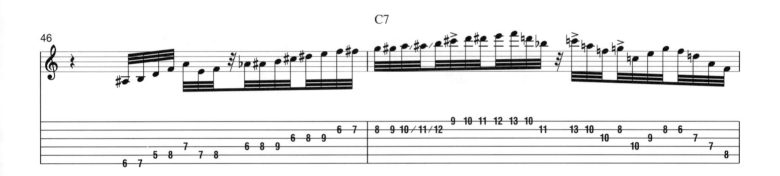

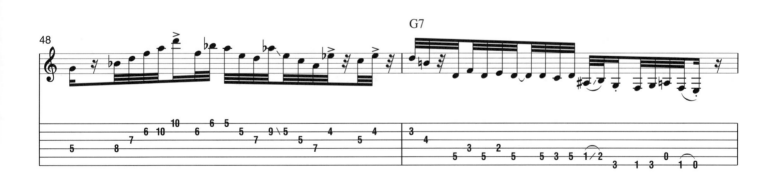

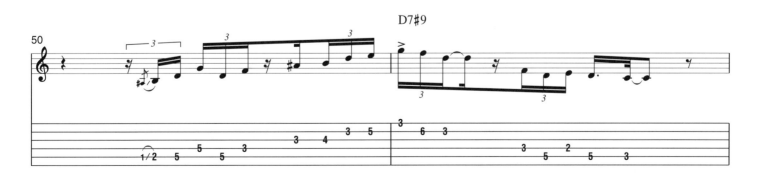

F Third Chorus

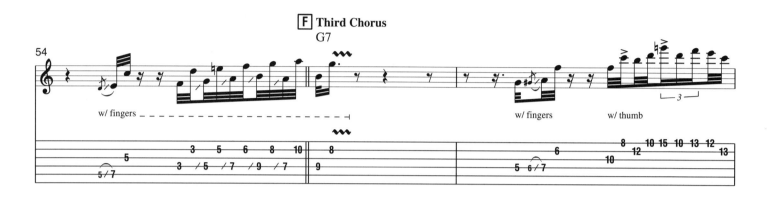

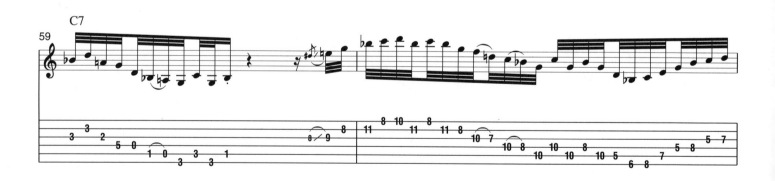

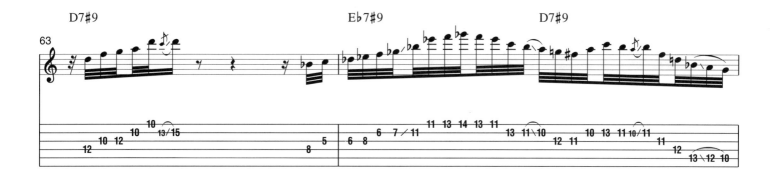

G Fourth Chorus

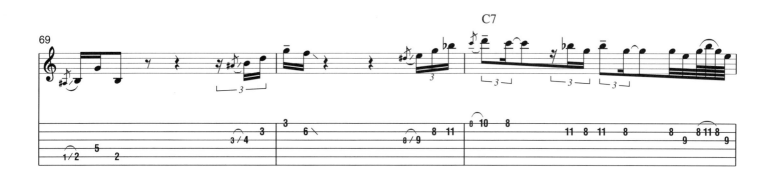

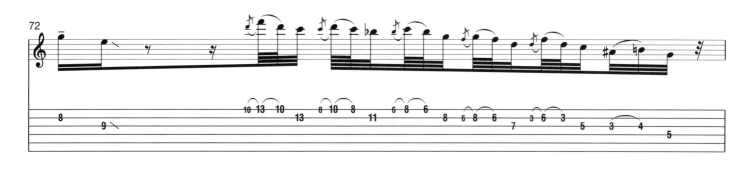

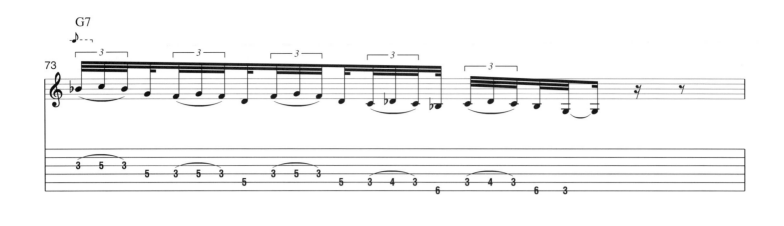

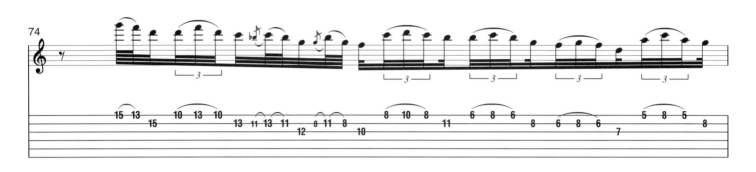

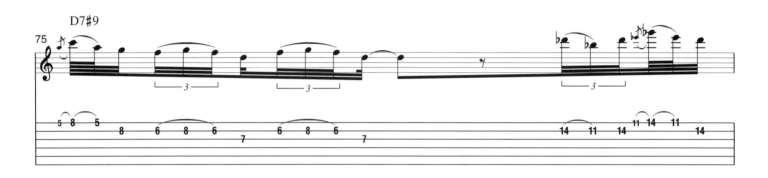

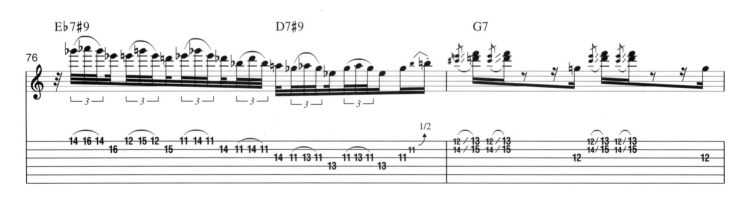

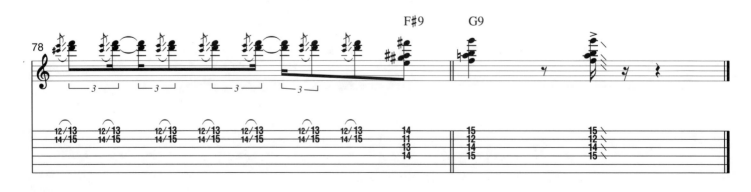

Kenny Burrell

Fig. 5 — Solo

Kenny Burrell is a consummate master of the blues in jazz. Countless players have borrowed and adapted his earthy licks; indeed these licks have become indispensable components of the jazz-guitar lexicon. Burrell's playing has always conveyed a distinct blues quality regardless of the ensemble, harmonic context, or type of composition. However, when actually playing a true blues tune, he is in a league of his own. It figures that his decision to include "All Blues" in the *Handcrafted* trio set would result in a soulful and fulfilling excursion.

Burrell has played in many settings and is quite effective in the piano-less trio format; this gives the guitar tremendous freedom harmonically, rhythmically, and melodically. His performance of "All Blues" finds him exploiting the trio ensemble for all its worth, freely mixing single-note lines and chord phrases in an inspired series of improvisations.

Personnel:	Trio. Kenny Burrell, guitar; Reggie Johnson, bass; Sherman Ferguson, drums.
Recorded:	February 28 or March 1,1978, at Dimension Sound, New York City.
Arrangement:	Burrell plays "All Blues" in the standard key of G at a moderate tempo, slightly faster than Benson's. This excerpt occurs at 2:44 in the track, which marks the beginning of his improvisations. Here, Burrell departs from the structured extensions and variations of the melody and is truly creating new material. He incorporates the song's central riff between solo phrases in [A] and [B]. A transition from straight 6/8 feel to swing occurs in [B] and is maintained for the remaining three choruses. The third chorus [C] is essentially chordal, while the final chorus [D] is played in single notes with chord punches.
Signatures:	Burrell uses a number of classic blues devices in his solo. In [A] and [B], he bases his improvised phrases around iterations of the core riff for an attractive *call-and-response* effect. This procedure also produces a nice balance of single-note versus chordal textures. Trademark bluesy double stops are played in measures 9, 11, 12, and 20. Burrell toys with the song's 6/8 meter throughout. He employs two-against-three cross-rhythms for licks in measures 15 and 43 and a similar hemiola-type syncopation for the D7#9–E♭7#9 chord phrase in measures 34–35.
Performance notes:	Most of Burrell's single-note lines are blues-oriented and based on the G Minor Pentatonic Scale or the G Blues Scale. Several key phrases indicate Burrell's preference for triplet note values in blues melody. His chord playing primarily makes use of the traditional 7th, 9th, 11th, and 13th chords of the blues genre. Many of his chord phrases are marked by half-step approach figures from above, as in measures 26, 29, 30, 36, and 42.
Sound:	Burrell's tone is usually produced by a Gibson Super 400 archtop electric with two humbuckers, or a D'Angelico New Yorker with a floating DeArmond pickup. He covers his f-holes with clear plastic tape to minimize acoustical feedback. Burrell uses medium picks. His main amp is a Fender Twin Reverb, though he occasionally plays through a Polytone.

7 Fig. 5

Moderate ♪ = 134

2:44

A First Chorus

* Tunes slightly flat (ca - 4 cts. A=436)
Track fades in one measure before music.
** Key signature denotes G Mixolydian.

B Second Chorus
Swing Feel

* Quick lift-off produces frethand mute.

let ring - - - -

Pat Martino

Fig. 6 — Solo

Though known primarily for his impressive output as a leader on Prestige, Cobblestone, Muse, Warner Brothers, and Blue Note labels, Pat Martino also excels in the sideman role. He came up through the ranks during the early 1960s playing in the East Coast organ-trio circuits, and was in high demand as an accompanist with giants like Jimmy Smith, Groove Holmes, Jack McDuff, and Don Patterson. Much of this superlative sideman work was captured on Prestige albums by Sonny Stitt, Charles McPherson, Willis Jackson, and Eric Kloss. "All Blues," from Eric Kloss's debut album, is precisely the sort of performance that formed a cornerstone of the Martino mythos.

"All Blues" yields one of Martino's finest sideman solos. It finds him in the familiar setting of organ trio plus saxophone. His role in the arrangement is largely that of a comping rhythm guitarist until his two-chorus solo spot. What ensues in those 24 bars is quite remarkable and one of Martino's most soulful and compelling blues improvisations on record.

Personnel: Quartet. Eric Kloss, alto saxophone; Pat Martino, guitar; Don Patterson, organ; Billy James, drums.

Recorded: Most likely November 1965, at Van Gelder Studios, Englewood Cliffs, New Jersey.

Arrangement: The Kloss arrangement is also played at a moderate tempo in the key of G. Martino solos in single notes over two choruses on the 12-bar form in A and B. Each chorus has its own feel. The first chorus A is in a straight 6/8 groove, and the second B is in a more animated swing feel.

Signatures: A prime identifier of Martino's style is the virtuosic single-note passagework which adorns much of his improvisation. This is clearly evident in "All Blues," with many hard bop melodies played in long streams of 32nd notes. These notes are delivered with Martino's equally identifiable unflagging sense of time and rhythmic placement. His florid lines are contrasted by traditional blues licks and modern intervallic and chromatic patterns. The pattern in measure 16 is a distinctive Martino motive from his early years. It is comprised of a three-note scale figure played in triplet rhythms and moved chromatically in half steps, here in descending motion. The phrase almost invariably appears as a transitional connective line.

Performance notes: Martino's practice of converting most scalar material to a minor-mode basis is in evidence throughout his solo. Though riddled with numerous chromatic passing tones and tension notes, the C7 lines in measures 5–6 are based on G minor, and the G7 melodies in 7–8 and 23–24 indicate D minor (melodic minor and Dorian mode). Martino plays a B♭m9 arpeggio over D7#9 in measures 21 and an A♭ minor bop line over E♭7#9 in measure 22— evidence of more exotic substitutions. In the first half of measure 23, he uses E♭ melodic minor (E♭–F–G♭–A♭–B♭–C–D) as a strong tension to imply the sound of a fully altered D7 chord resolving to G7. Martino completes this complex harmonic maneuver by simply moving E♭ minor to D minor—an innate advantage of his minor conversion concept. Precision and clarity have been hallmarks of the Martino style since his earliest recordings. His virtuosic lines are made all the more attractive with the precise picking and well-accented articulation he employs. Like his role models, Wes Montgomery and Johnny Smith, Martino favors a linear approach involving fluid position-shifting in the course of long bebop lines.

Sound: On the original recording, Martino played a Gibson Les Paul Custom through a Fender Twin Reverb amp. This info was recently confirmed for me by Pat himself. Shortly after the Kloss session, Martino's Les Paul was stolen and he replaced it with a series of Gibson archtop electrics, including an ES-175, and several L-5s.

8 Fig. 6

[A] **First Chorus**

Moderately ♪ = 132-134 Triplet Feel

* Key signature denotes G Mixolydian.

SO WHAT
By Miles Davis

"So What," the second Miles Davis offering in this volume, also comes from the monumental *Kind of Blue* album. This phase of Davis's music has been referred to as his modal period, largely because of this composition. Its effect on the subsequent wave of jazz was both enormous and far-reaching, attracting musicians from the most conservative to the most avant-garde. "So What" is a 32-bar AABA form based on 16 measures of one scale, eight of another, and eight more of the first. The original recording featured an antiphonal call-and-response arrangement of the theme in which a bass melody was answered by horn ensemble figures. This treatment is an identifier of the piece and is handled in two distinctly different ways by Barney Kessel and George Benson. Both players further enlarge on the piece in their signature solos.

Barney Kessel

Fig. 7 — Head and Solo

Barney Kessel was the most recognized jazz guitarist of the late 1950s, and was among the first of the Charlie Christian disciples to define the guitar sound of the next era. Born in Muskogee, Oklahoma, he began playing at the age of 12, and is largely self-taught. Kessel came up in the1940s big bands of Charlie Barnet and Artie Shaw and combos such as the Gramercy Five and the stellar Oscar Peterson trio of 1952. He is further renowned for his appearances with Norman Granz's Jazz at the Philharmonic series, which included Lester Young and Ella Fitzgerald. Kessel's versatility allowed him to enjoy a dual career as jazz musician and studio player. In the latter vein, he recorded with artists like Elvis Presley, the Beach Boys, T-Bone Walker, Cher, Judy Garland, Duane Eddy, and Frank Sinatra, and added his guitarwork to many TV and film soundtracks. In the late 1950s, Kessel consistently topped the readers polls in *Down Beat, Metronome,* and *Playboy* magazines. He joined forces with kindred spirits Ray Brown and Shelly Manne in a trio collectively named The Pollwinners. The group produced highly inventive, swinging jazz as evidenced by the 1960 recording *The Pollwinners Exploring the Scene* and their version of "So What."

This is a superb reinterpretation of the Davis classic. The Pollwinners transplant Davis's larger ensemble arrangement of the piece into a trio setting yet maintain the intent and feel of the original. Though lighter in sonic density, "So What" cooks unerringly from its opening notes. This excerpt presents the head and Kessel's two-chorus solo.

Personnel: Trio. Barney Kessel, guitar; Ray Brown, bass; Shelly Manne, drums and percussion.

Recorded: August 30, 31, or September 1, 1960, at Contemporary Records studio, Los Angeles, California.

Arrangement: Like the original Miles Davis track, the Pollwinners play "So What" at a moderate tempo in D minor. The head [A] is a trio rendering of the melody stated by the bass and answered first by an odd percussion instrument, a lujon or mbira, and then by Kessel's chord figures. The latter are paraphrases of the original horn phrases. Following the 32-bar head, the groove changes to a slightly faster swing feel and Kessel solos in [B] and [C] over two choruses of the form.

Signatures: Kessel plays with a horn-like concept in single-note improvisation, often running strings of swung eighth notes in the manner of a saxophonist. The simulation of a horn style has been the jazz-guitar paradigm since Charlie Christian's breakthrough in 1939. The idiosyncratic slurred and raked figures in measures 58–61 are a well-known Kessel identifier, as is the swinging and highly rhythmic chord work in [C]. Another identifier is Kessel's strong swing feel, which permeates his improvisations.

Performance notes: Kessel divides his solo texturally. The first chorus [B] is played in single notes and the second [C] is played in chords. Most of his lines in [B] are in eighth-note values, befitting the swing and early bebop style. As is common in modal jazz, many of Kessel's melodies are based on extended D minor and E♭ minor arpeggios, emphasizing the mildly dissonant, upper chord tones: 9ths, 11ths, and 13ths. This is particularly evident in measures 35–43, 55, and 58–61. The slurred figures in measures 58–61 are played with both ascending and descending sweep picking and are depictive of the smeared note effect of jazz saxophone applied to guitar. Kessel's emblematic *thumb fretting* technique is used to play G11 and A♭11 chords in measures 73–88.

Sound: Kessel has played virtually the same guitar since the 1950s. This is a modified Gibson ES-350 arch-top with a single Charlie Christian bar pickup and a dot-inlay fingerboard. He has used various Gibson, Fender and Univox amps over the years. Kessel uses a heavy pick and Darco medium-heavy gauge roundwound strings.

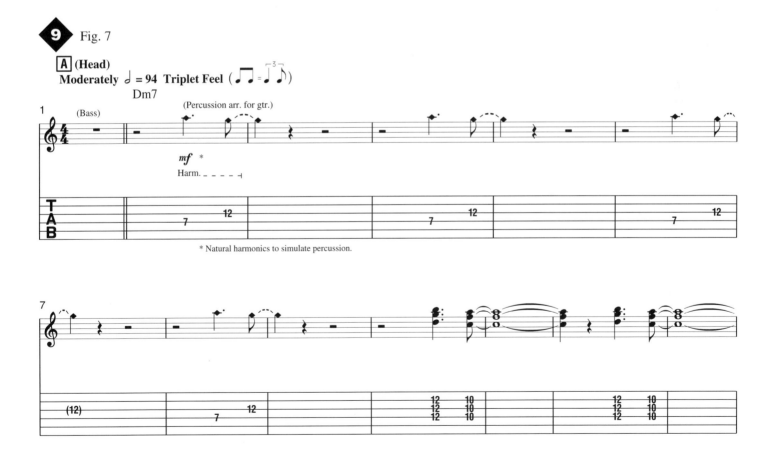

* G stg. sounds accidentally

George Benson

Fig. 8 — Intro and Head
Fig. 9 — Solo

George Benson's career as a solo jazz artist soared during his association with Creed Taylor's CTI records. In addition to many releases as a leader, he recorded with the likes of Freddie Hubbard, Herbie Hancock, and Miles Davis. Initially marketed as a successor to the Wes Montgomery throne, Benson took the post-Montgomery legacy to the next level and beyond. Appropriately titled, the *Beyond the Blue Horizon* record of 1972 epitomized his expansion of the jazz-guitar art form. On this album, Benson was captured as a highly individual and distinctive instrumentalist coming out of the Montgomery tradition, but was not stereotyped or limited by its trappings. No recording from this era better demonstrates that fact or embodies the contribution as convincingly as Benson's rendition of "So What."

Benson's "So What" is a hard-driving reinterpretation of the jazz classic. It stands as a career milestone and showcases his talents as both a formidable straight-ahead jazz guitarist and a funky player with a command of rock and blues idioms. The tune's static harmonic structure leaves plenty of room for exploration, elaboration, and substitution, which Benson utilizes to the fullest extent.

Personnel: Quartet. George Benson, guitar; Clarence Palmer, organ; Ron Carter, bass; Jack DeJohnette, drums.

Recorded: February 2 or 3, 1971, at Van Gelder Studios, Englewood Cliffs, New Jersey.

Arrangement: Benson also plays "So What" in the standard key of D minor at a moderate tempo. He has made several significant modifications to the tune, the most obvious being the tunes opening rock groove, maintained for the intro [A] and head [B]. Benson plays a truncated version of the melody in measures 8-20. He states the complete melody using the guitar's lower register in [B] answered by the organ punching the songs familiar chord bursts. The solo sections alternate feels and tempo in this fashion: rock feel [C] and [F], fast swing [D] and [G], and medium swing [E] and [H], to produce a constantly changing six-chorus form.

Signatures: Benson's solo contains a mix of funky jazz-rock and blues-based licks with heady bebop phrases. It is a predominately single-note solo with smaller chord riffs in [F] and [H]. Benson generally tempers his ideas and adjusts his phrasing to reflect the mood of each chorus and its distinct feel. The first chorus [C] is distinguished by pentatonic/blues scale flurries and straightforward lines from the Dorian mode. The second [D] exposes the bebop side of Benson's playing with more elaborate jazz melodies. Most of Benson's bop phrases are arranged as long eighth-note groupings, as in measures 20–28, 35–40, 80–86, and 87–95. The third chorus [E] exploits bluesy triplet rhythms, groove riffs, and a climactic slurred phrase. The fourth [F] returns to a rock feel with shorter fragmented licks, and establishes funky double stops as a texture and thematic element that is heard again in [H]. These two-note figures are made funkier with Benson's use of muting and *rhythmic displacement*. The fifth chorus [G] elaborates on his earlier bebop lines and contains a dramatic across-the-barline trill in measures 112–113. The final chorus [H] is riff-dominated, complete with blues licks and an ostinato based on slurred three-note chords in measures 118–125. This chordal device is frequently used by Benson to create tension and exciting climaxes in his solos.

Performance notes: When playing modal tunes based on a stationary harmonic structure, most jazz musicians often depart from the strict use of one particular scale during a solo. Benson's departures include substitutions, as well as "outside" (out of the basic tonal center) playing. Superimposed chord sounds can be heard variously as A7♭9(♯5) in measures 21–22 and 84–85, Bm7♭5 in measure 23, Cmaj7 in measures 26–27, B♭m7 in measure 87, and Fm(maj9) in measure 92—all over D minor. The all-important bebop motive of G–F–D–D♯–E is an identifier of a mature jazz player, i.e., one who has absorbed the vocabulary of influential alto saxophonist Charlie Parker. This "Parker lick" is heard throughout the mainstream jazz genre. It occurs in Benson's solo, on varied pitch levels, in measures 14, 39, 50, 84–85, 91, 94–95, and 103. Illustrative examples of Benson's inside-outside-inside lines are found in measures 6–7, 11–13, 52–54, 69–71, and 86–88.

Sound: On the original album cover, Benson is pictured with a Guild Artist Award archtop equipped with a floating DeArmond-type pickup. Benson generally favored Fender Twin Reverb amps during this period.

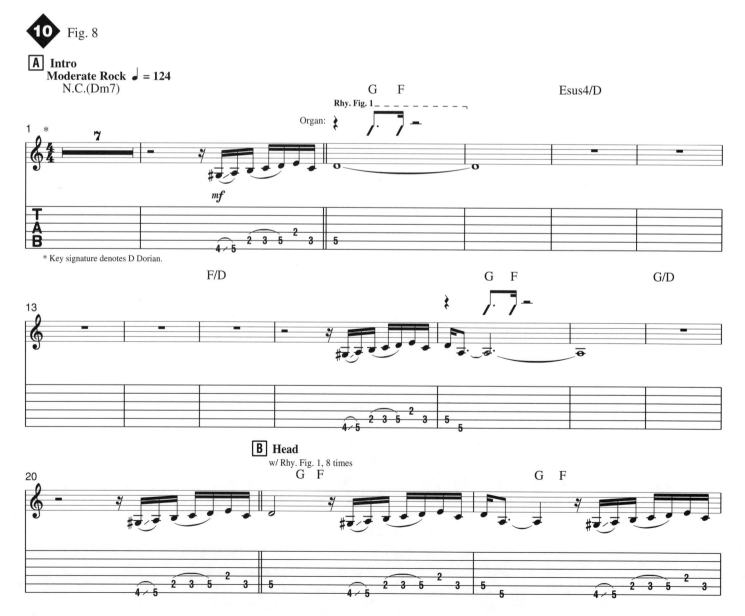

10 Fig. 8

A Intro
Moderate Rock ♩ = 124

* Key signature denotes D Dorian.

B Head
w/ Rhy. Fig. 1, 8 times

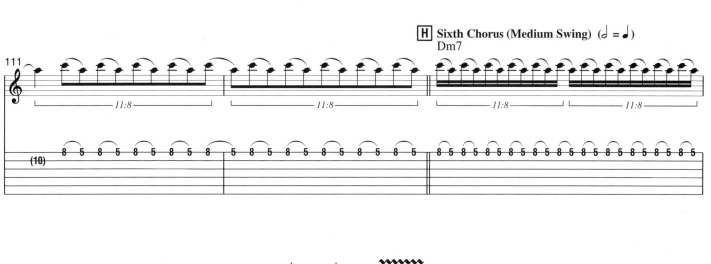

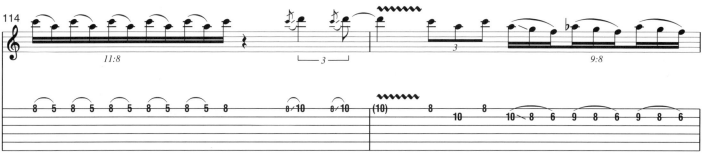

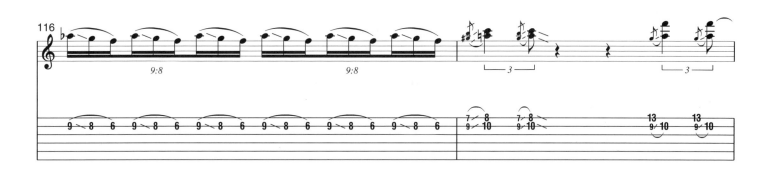

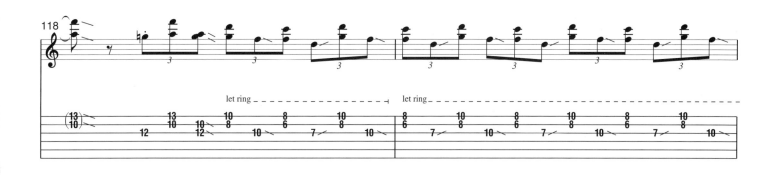

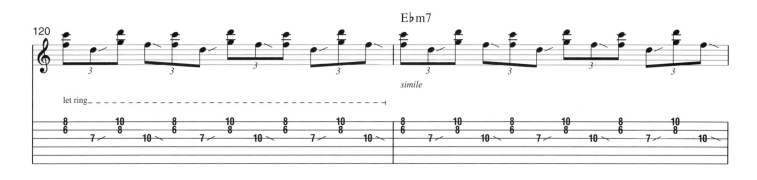

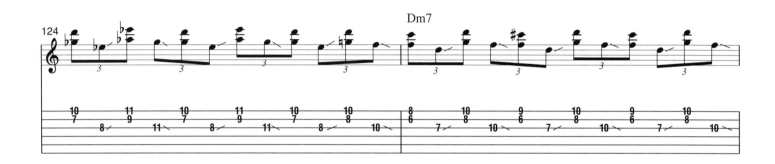

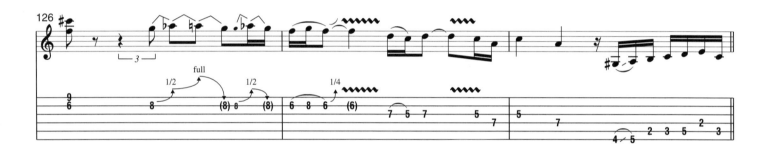

G Interlude
Rock Feel

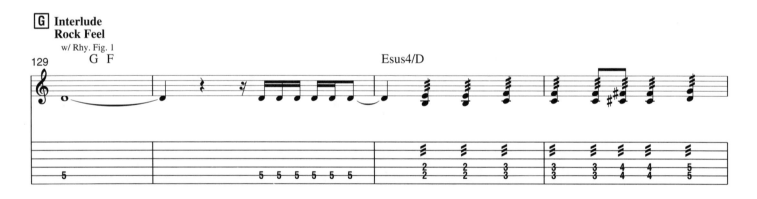

* Trem pick w/ steady gliss.

ALL THE THINGS YOU ARE
Lyrics by Oscar Hammerstein II   Music by Jerome Kern

Much of the mainstream jazz repertory is based on show tunes used as vehicles for rearrangement, elaboration, and improvisation. These utilitarian compositions came to be called *standards* by jazz musicians. One of the most famous and often-recorded standards is "All the Things You Are"—a popular song written in 1939 by composer Jerome Kern and since covered by countless jazz players including guitarists Wes Montgomery, Howard Roberts, Jim Hall, Tal Farlow, Grant Green, and Jimmy Bruno. "All the Things You Are" is set in a 36-bar song form symbolized as AABA (8+8+8+12) and exploits a frequently-used chord progression known as the cycle of fourths. Two interesting and contrasting treatments of the standard come to the repertory via Hank Garland and Pat Metheny.

Hank Garland

Fig. 10 — Head and Solo

Hank "Sugarfoot" Garland is an artist of remarkable breadth, versatility, and musicality. His career has been multi-faceted. He has been able to effectively contribute to the disparate worlds of country and western and jazz as well as rock 'n' roll and pop. Garland was born in Cowpens, South Carolina, and was drawn at an early age to the indigenous country music of the area. He began playing guitar at age six, and turned professional by his adolescent years. Garland was one of the first pickers to overturn the Grand Ole Opry's long-standing boycott of electric guitars and soon became one of the leading instrumentalists in the prominent Nashville session scene of the 1950s. During this period, he recorded with such luminaries as Elvis Presley, Roy Orbison, the Everly Brothers and Patsy Cline. Always an innovator, he further broke more new ground by turning his prodigious talents to the jazz genre. It was in Nashville in 1960 that Garland recorded the landmark jazz guitar album *Jazz Winds from a New Direction*. *Jazz Winds* has endured the test of time and proved influential to countless players including George Benson and Jimmy Bruno.

"All the Things You Are," an outstanding track on the *Jazz Winds* album, received a scintillating treatment. In addition to the impressive technique and strong bebop conception of Garland's improvised solo choruses, the piece boasted a unique arrangement and an uncommon ensemble setting.

Personnel: Quartet. Hank Garland, guitar; Gary Burton, vibes; Joe Benjamin, bass; Joe Morello, drums.

Recorded: June 23, 1960, at Columbia Studios, Nashville, Tennessee.

Arrangement: Garland plays "All the Things You Are" uptempo in the standard key of A-flat. His arrangement, however, is hardly standard. The head [A] combines two feels: a baroque-style fugal rendering of the A sections with a double-time swing feel in B sections and behind solos. Garland plays imitative single-note counterlines to the vibe melody in the A sections and comps rhythmically behind the vibe melody in the bridge. He begins his improvisations with a two-bar break in measures 35–36 and takes two choruses of the 36-bar form for his solo in [B] and [C].

Signatures: Garland's solo is distinguished by a swinging, Tal Farlow-inspired approach. His single-note lines—predominately in eighth-note rhythms—beautifully outline the chord changes and are often played as long bebop-oriented steams, as found in measures 35–40, 49–52, 56–61, 77–80, 82–85, and 102–104. These bebop lines contain both extended arpeggio outlines (spelling 9th, 11th, and 13th chords) and linear melodies incorporating chromaticism. Garland superimposes the sophisticated sound of the Lydian mode over tonic major seventh chords in measures 43, 64, and 87. He adds country and blues inflections to his jazz lines in measures 51–54, 74–76, and 79–80.

Performance notes: Garland's ideas and swing feel are of the highest order, as is his technique. Regarding the latter, his fluid and seamless position changing within a string of fast eighth notes is the quintessence of bebop guitar. Many of his phrases include a characteristic jazz line often called the "Honeysuckle Rose lick". Associated with bop horn players, this lick is derived from the "Honeysuckle Rose" melody (see Fig. 12). It has three distinct components: a downward whole step and leap of a minor sixth, followed by an ascending minor arpeggio, and then descending scalar or chromatic motion. Beyond a cliche, it is a vital piece of the mature bop player's vocabulary. In Garland's solo, the lick occurs in measures 58, 69, 84, 94, and 99–100, and frequently involves a position change in the midst of a long and complex string of eighth notes.

Sound: Garland played a custom thin-body Gibson L-5 with a Charlie Christian bar pickup on this date. According to brother Billy Garland, Hank rewound these pickups by hand to produce a thicker, rounder tone. He strung his guitar with Gibson 240 medium-gauge strings and employed heavy picks. Though he regularly played through a Gibson amp, for this session Garland used a Fender Pro amp with one 15-inch speaker.

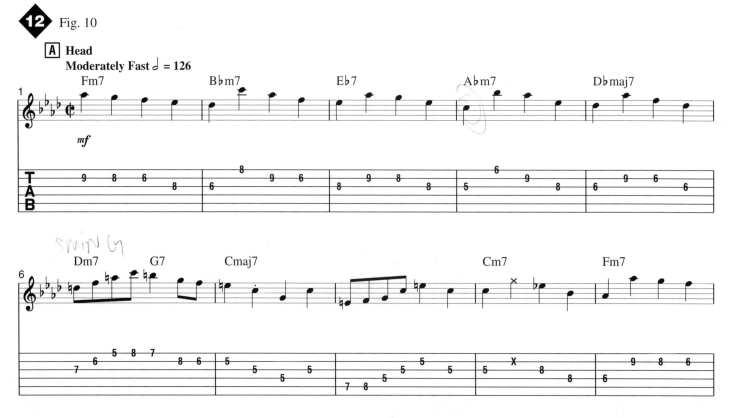

Pat Metheny

Fig. 11 — Head and Solo

Pat Metheny is representative of the "new school" of jazz guitar. Born in Lee's Summit, Missouri, Metheny was raised in the Kansas City area, and was originally inspired by Wes Montgomery, Jim Hall, Miles Davis, and Ornette Coleman. He attended Boston's Berklee School of Music and the University of Miami. Metheny came to prominence in the 1970s ECM wave of jazz, initially through his work on (vibist) Gary Burton's records. Interestingly, Burton played on Hank Garland's *Jazz Winds* which yielded an earlier important guitar-led version of "All the Things You Are." (See Fig. 10) Metheny made a name for himself and built a tremendous following through his own ECM recordings. He became a "jazz star" by the 1980s, and, by virtue of his cross-over jazz/rock style, worked with many diverse artists in unusual settings, including Joni Mitchell, Ornette Coleman, Paul Simon, and Derek Bailey. By the end of the 1980s, Metheny's sound and style defined a genre. A rare departure from Metheny's usual tightly-structured releases mainly comprised of originals, 1990's *Question and Answer* was loose and spontaneous. In the spirit of a mainstream jazz album, it was recorded with a no-frills attitude in a single eight-hour session and contained several standards, including "All the Things You Are."

Metheny's modern treatment of "All the Things You Are" is perhaps the most straight-ahead reading of anything he has produced. This is jazz—Metheny style. The head and four choruses of soloing are offered in this depictive excerpt.

Personnel: Trio. Pat Metheny, guitar; Dave Holland, bass; Roy Haynes, drums.

Recorded: December 21, 1989, at Power Station, New York City.

Arrangement: Metheny also plays the tune in the standard key, A-flat. Taken at a fast tempo, his arrangement is more straightforward than Garland's: He states the head in single notes in A. The tune's melody receives a characteristic syncopated Metheny treatment. The solo, as in Garland's arrangement, begins with a break in measures 35–36, and is also played in single notes.

Signatures: Hallmarks of Metheny's style include the use of specific motives—melodic, harmonic, and rhythmic—and other thematic figures developed during improvisation. His approach is highly rhythmic, and exploits syncopation and across-the-barline phrasing as deliberate devices. Another aspect is his highly identifiable sound, mostly produced with legato phrasing. Metheny's sound and articulation are of the jazz archtop tradition, though somewhat removed from the mainstream (Montgomery, Pass, Burrell) in that he favors a more processed electric tone and a more dissonant harmonic language. Many of his lines go beyond conventional jazz harmonic substitution and are representative of the post-bebop style of *action jazz*.

Performance notes: Metheny mixes sequential melodious phrases with two- or three-measure eighth-note flurries and longer streams of eighth notes in his solo. Sequences based on melodic fragments are found in measures 37–49, 55–59, 102–104, 109–116, and 173–177. These are contrasted by eighth-note strings in measures 85–91, 96–100, 132–136, 140–151, 169–172, and 177–181. Many of these lines incorporate chromaticism freely. The phrase first heard in measures 51–52 is recalled as a variant in measures 88, 100, 123–124, 142, and 158–159.

Fourth intervals occur in measures 66–67. Atonality is heard in measures 133–135, 143–145, and 170–173. Though Metheny's "outside" melodies may owe more stylistically to Ornette Coleman and Eric Dolphy than Charlie Parker or Dizzy Gillespie, his eighth-note phrasing still alludes to the pioneering horn-based concepts of Charlie Christian and his disciples. He even inserts a fragmentary Christian motif in measure 101, as if to reinforce the connection, as far-fetched as it may seem in this context.

Sound: The Metheny sound is more processed than most jazz guitarists. It is usually obtained with an archtop electric—most often his trademark blond Gibson ES-175—and an Acoustic 134 combo amp. Reverb, delay, and chorus are often added via a Lexicon unit. On this session date, Metheny's ES-175 was overseas prompting him to use his newly-designed Ibanez Pat Metheny model.

13 Fig. 11

* Signature licks track fades out.

HONEYSUCKLE ROSE

Words by Andy Razaf   Music by Thomas "Fats" Waller

Fats Waller was one of the earliest and most influential performer-composers in jazz. A notable pianist of the stride tradition, he married the jazz sensibilities of the 1920s with the pop style of Tin Pan Alley. "Honeysuckle Rose" is a durable Waller milestone embodying this marriage. A catchy song set in a 32-bar AABA form, it is one of the most recorded tunes in jazz history and has served as a vehicle for Charlie Parker, Coleman Hawkins, Gerry Mulligan, and many others. Two unique contrasting guitar approaches to "Honeysuckle Rose" are presented by the Joe Pass/Herb Ellis duo and the immortal Charlie Christian.

Joe Pass and Herb Ellis

Fig. 12 — Head and Solos

The jazz guitar duet has a venerable lineage as old as the history of jazz itself. Among the earliest duo recordings were those of Eddie Lang and Lonnie Johnson in the late 1920s. These were followed by the teams of Carl Kress/Dick McDonough and Frank Victor/Harry Volpe in the 1930s, Carl Kress/Tony Mottola and Carmen Mastren/Albert Harris in the 1940s, John Pisano/Billy Bean in the 1950s, and George Barnes/Bucky Pizzarelli in the 1960s. The jazz guitar duet reached an apex with the pairing of Joe Pass and Herb Ellis. Each was a seasoned exponent of mainstream jazz with a wealth of experience and a strong individual voice on the instrument. Their union proved to be one of the most compelling and successful in the jazz-guitar duo tradition. On their debut Concord recording, Pass and Ellis chose a fine array of standards as vehicles; this array included the timeless "Honeysuckle Rose," which received a gorgeous duet treatment.

The Pass/Ellis duo performed "Honeysuckle Rose" at a slow tempo, as Fats Waller intended. Infinitely malleable, the tune in this setting becomes the ideal environment for sensitive interaction, spontaneous counterpoint, and sheer guitar beauty.

Personnel: Duet. Joe Pass and Herb Ellis, guitars.

Recorded: 1972, at Wally Heider Studios, Los Angeles, California.

Arrangement: Pass and Ellis play "Honeysuckle Rose" in the original key of F at a slow tempo. Their arrangement is the epitome of interaction. They utilize a "head chart" approach—no music is necessary (just ears)—because both players know the tune intimately and are making up the arrangement and variations as they play. Herb (Gtr.1) takes the lead in the A sections $\boxed{A}$, $\boxed{B}$, and $\boxed{D}$, passing it over to Joe (Gtr.2), in the B section $\boxed{C}$.

Signatures: Beyond its importance in the jazz repertory as a perennial standard, "Honeysuckle Rose" is noted for its distinctive A section theme dubbed the *Honeysuckle Rose lick* (bracketed in the transcription). This familiar melody has transcended the confines of the tune to become an essential melodic component of the jazz language. Ellis delivers the theme melody in single notes with his typically elegant phrasing, coloring it with blues licks, soulful vibrato, and chromatic ornamentation. Pass accompanies Ellis with his familiar pianistic chord-melody style in the A sections. Their roles reverse in the bridge. The Pass-Ellis duo represents a microcosm of jazz guitar history with Ellis summing up the post-Charlie Christian blues/swing style and Pass exemplifying the post-Wes Montgomery hard-bop style. However, such designations blur in episodes like the closing phrases of measures 15–16 and 31–32, where the interweaving single-note lines culminate in uncanny spontaneous jazz counterpoint.

Performance notes: Ellis plays with a pick to squarely articulate single-note melodies and to arpeggiate his "accompanimental" chord figures in the bridge. Ellis's 10th-voiced strummed chord forms in measures 19–20 are a staple of swing jazz rhythm guitar (a la Freddie Green) and also allude to the stride-piano tradition. Note that these voicings have a muted inner string (marked by Xs) to accommodate the strummed attack. By contrast, Pass solely plays with his fingers. This chord-melody style is reminiscent of his work as an accompanist, and on solo records such as the *Virtuoso* series. He uses his fingers to articulate single-note melodies in the bridge and favors a legato approach to phrasing lines, as found in the ascending flurry in measure 22.

Sound: Attesting further to its reputation as the workingman's jazz box, both Ellis and Pass play Gibson ES-175s. Ellis's model is a 1954 with a single P-90 pickup. He strung it with Darco flat-wound strings (he currently uses Thomastik-Infeld flats) and uses a heavy pick. Pass's 175 is an early 1960s model with dual humbuckers. Amplification is low and minimal. At this point, Ellis played through a Benson or Emrad, and Pass plugged into a Polytone.

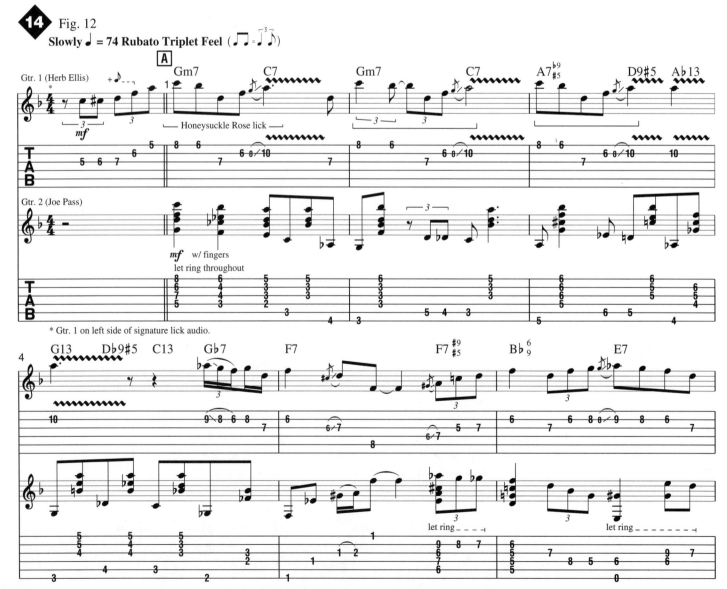

14 Fig. 12

Slowly ♩ = 74 Rubato Triplet Feel

72

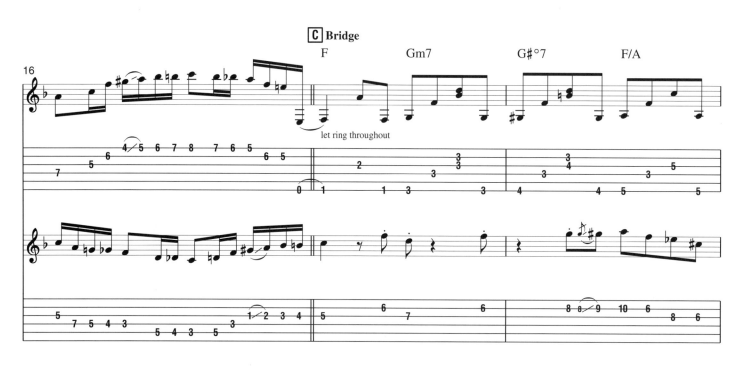

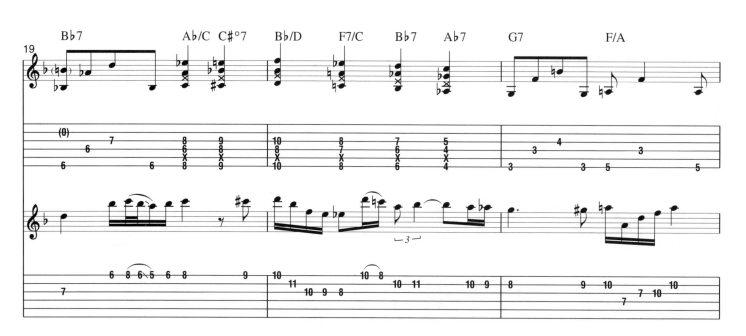

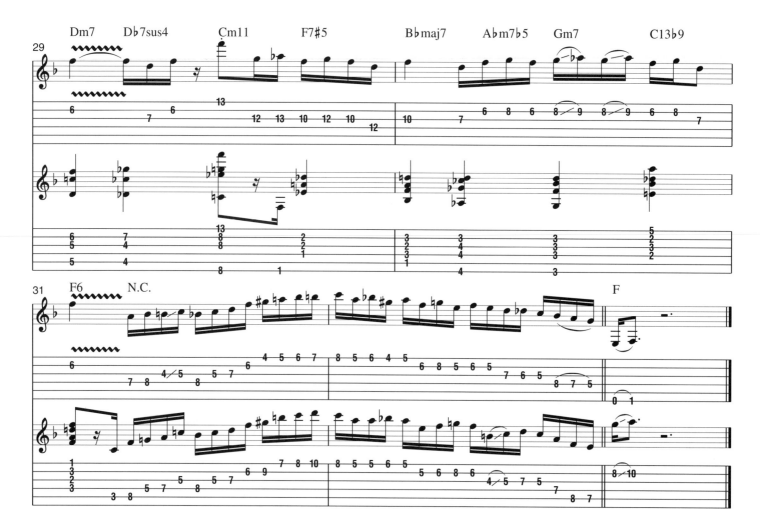

Charlie Christian

Fig. 13 — Solo

Charlie Christian is universally acknowledged as the father of modern jazz guitar. Christian was the principal role model for jazz guitarists worldwide—his solos were learned note-for-note, and his sound, phrasing, and articulation were emulated and appeared in varied forms with his successors. Following his appearance and short career (1939-1942), a school of stylistic disciples emerged and spread his influence far and wide. Charlie Christian was born in 1912 in Bonham, Texas, and raised in the Oklahoma City area. He was introduced to the electric guitar by Eddie Durham in 1937. By 1938, Christian was touring the Midwest as an electric guitarist and developing a regional following with Alphonso Trent's Septet. Impresario John Hammond learned of Christian through the grapevine and hooked him up with swing king Benny Goodman. The rest is history. During his association with Goodman, Christian became one of the biggest names of the swing era. Not content to rest on his laurels and merely enjoy the fruits of his stardom, he pushed the envelope further. In 1940, Christian was part of the milieu at Minton's Playhouse in Harlem, and foreshadowed the arrival of the bebop idiom along with early practitioners Dizzy Gillespie, Thelonius Monk, and Kenny Clarke.

"Honeysuckle Rose" is a milestone solo in guitar lore. The outing exemplifies the early role of Christian's electric guitar in big-band jazz of the swing era. For the first time in history, a guitarist was granted a prominent solo spot equivalent to those previously only given to sax and trumpet soloists.

Personnel: The 15-piece Benny Goodman Orchestra with Charlie Christian on guitar.

Recorded: November 22, 1939, in New York City, NY.

Arrangement:	Goodman's arrangement is in the key of D-flat (better suited to the big band ensemble) and played uptempo. Christian plays background rhythm until his solo spot at 1:15 into the tune. There he takes one full chorus of the 32-bar form.

Signatures: Christian's licks became the lingua franca of the first epoch of jazz guitar, and this solo contains many of those notable aspects of his single-note style. These include longer strings of swung eighth notes alternating with shorter rhythmic motives and blues-based phrases. The rising Ab13 arpeggio in measure 1 is a favorite melodic formula and appears in many contexts in Christian's playing. The phrase in measures 19–20 contains another favorite melodic formula—this time for a major chord. It rises with a Gb major arpeggio, descends with a chromatic line, and ends with a descending Gb6 arpeggio. Many of Christian's longer 8th-note phrases include this pattern. He uses a dramatic octave-skipping melody in measures 25–27. Strong rhythmic punctuation and syncopation emphasize the wide interval leaps of an octave and major 7th. Christian's closing lines contain distinct blues inflections, including a long string bend in measure 30 that is gradually released in measure 31.

Performance notes: Christian's physical technique was observed and described by Barney Kessel this way: "He played probably 95 percent downstrokes, and held a very stiff, big triangular pick very tightly between his thumb and first finger. He rested his second, third, and fourth fingers very firmly on the pickguard. He almost never used the fourth finger of his left hand."

Sound: The tone Christian pioneered remains the classic "jazz guitar sound" to the present. Christian played, or more accurately *immortalized,* the Gibson ES-150. This was the first *Electric Spanish* guitar: a non-cutaway archtop guitar fitted with a single bar pickup. Through his use, the bar pickup became known as the "Charlie Christian pickup" and was the standard for most jazz guitarists in the 1940s and 1950s. Barney Kessel and Hank Garland use them to this day. Christian used both the 15-watt EH-150 as well as the more powerful (18 watts) EH-185 amp.

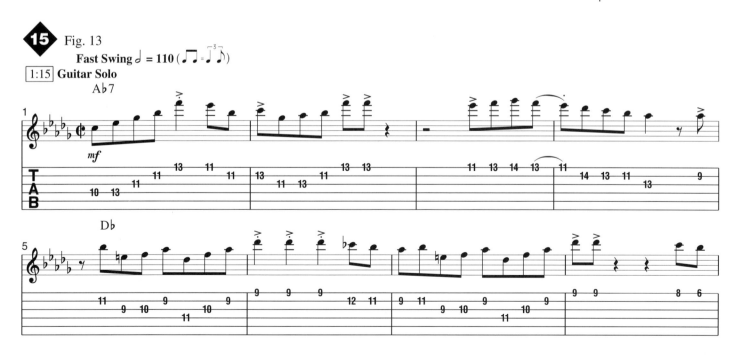

SATIN DOLL

By Duke Ellington

The legendary bandleader Duke Ellington was one of the most important composers of the 20th century, and "Satin Doll" is arguably his most familiar song. A true standard that sprang from the heart of jazz, it has been played and recorded frequently and is now firmly embedded in the repertory of contemporary music. Set in a 32-bar AABA form, "Satin Doll" is distinguished by a breezy melody that brings out the best in chord-melody stylists of the guitar and a set of changes that has enticed countless players to construct their own memorable variations on Ellington's theme. Two cases in point are the sparkling renditions by Howard Roberts and Joe Pass.

Howard Roberts

Fig. 14 — Head, Solo, Interlude, and Outro

Howard Roberts was a remarkably eclectic jazz guitarist. An adventurous and scholarly musician, HR walked a musical tightrope for most of his professional life, dividing his time between pop and rock recording sessions and a career as a solo artist. Born in Phoenix, Arizona, Roberts received his musical training in the local jazz and blues clubs and turned pro by 15. He moved to Los Angeles in 1950 and became entrenched in the city's jazz scene. Through Barney Kessel, HR met guitarist-arranger-producer Jack Marshall, who helped him secure touring dates and later studio work. He began making a name for himself as a jazz artist with a Verve Records contract in the mid-1950s, and solidified that reputation with his popular Capitol recordings of the 1960s. Simultaneously, HR played on many landmark studio recordings for film and TV that are now part of Americana—most notably the themes to "The Twilight Zone," "M*A*S*H," and "The Beverly Hillbillies." His work also took him into the 1960s rock realm. Roberts appeared on so many Monkees records he was dubbed the "fifth Monkee." At last count, he had cut more than 5,000 tracks as a sideman, and made over 20 albums as a leader. Commercial work did nothing to impair HR's ability as a jazz guitarist; rather, it colored his music with an unusual modern tinge—apparent in tunes like "Satin Doll."

"Satin Doll" is one of the most straight-ahead recordings from HR's Capitol period. It finds him in the favored setting of a funky organ-based quartet—an ensemble that brings out his most hard-driving, blues-oriented jazz playing.

Personnel:	Quartet. Howard Roberts, guitar; Burkley Kendrix, organ; Chuck Berghoffer, bass; Earl Palmer, drums.
Recorded:	June or July, 1963, at Capitol Records Studio A, Hollywood, California.
Arrangement:	Roberts plays "Satin Doll" in the standard key of C. Typical of his Capitol period, HR's arrangement is concise but eventful. He renders the A sections in *block-chord style.* The eight-bar bridge melody is played in single notes and treated ad lib: implied with an intervallic line and stated outright in only two measures: 24 and 25. HR's solo choruses, measures 35–50 and 59–66, are played over the A changes. The organ solos over the bridge. An eight-bar interlude $\boxed{\text{D}}$, based on the bridge changes, provides a segue back to a statement of the A section $\boxed{\text{E}}$. This recap and a four-bar tag concludes the arrangement. HR plays one of his famous closing cadenzas in measures 86-89.
Signatures:	Roberts possessed one of the most facile and swinging block-chord styles in jazz. Heard in the head of "Satin Doll," it is an

outgrowth of the early (pre-polyphonic) George Van Eps plectrum-based approach. HR's choice of harmonies reflects a penchant for the blues, particularly in his use of parallel 13th and 9th chords in measures 7–8, 15–16, 31–32, 79–80, and 83–84. These are spiced up with slurs and his trademark tremolo in measures 15–16. The solo epitomizes Roberts's single-note style: an amalgam of funky blues licks mixed with bebop and swing lines offset by unpredictable intervallic melodies enhanced by his uncommon phrasing. Folksy blues licks are found in measures 33–34, 60–62, and 65–66. These are contrasted by more complex 16th-note bop lines in measures 36–39 and 44–47. Wide intervallic leaps are exploited in measures 19–22, and worked into lines in measures 47 and notably in 49. HR plays a favorite motive, "The Django lick," in measure 45. This phrase, borrowed from Django Rheinhardt, has become a mainstay of jazz. It is an ascending pattern constructed of four-note groups based on an arpeggio shape and is usually played in 16th notes. Here HR outlines a tonic C major arpeggio with the *"Django lick."* HR's cadenza utilizes a G major scale played over the final Cmaj9 chord. This is one of Robert's favorite sounds (major 7th with a raised 11th—Lydian mode) and occurs often in his style.

Performance notes: HR employs a legato approach to strummed block chords, generally striving for a smooth connected sound in changes. This is facilitated by *economy fingering* exemplified in the interlude chord riffs. Here, the Dm triad (used as an upper partial of Gm9: beat 4, measure 67) is fingered with ring-middle-index and is maintained "under" the next chord, C6/9 (beat 1, measure 68), which is fingered with a pinky barre on the first and second strings and the ring finger on the third string, and is played again without re-fingering on beat 2. Robert's longer bebop phrases require several characteristic position changes, most explicit in measures 46–47. Many of these tricky shifts are accomplished by sliding on the half steps, a technique HR revealed in his pedagogy of the early 1970s.

Sound: Roberts played a one-of-a-kind, highly modified archtop electric guitar on "Satin Doll" and throughout the 1960s and 1970s. (See photo in Axology.) Previously owned by Herb Ellis, it began as a late-1930s Gibson ES-150. HR changed its shape, fingerboard and neck, electronics, and finish. By the mid-'60s Roberts used a 50-watt Benson 300HR combo amp fitted with a 12-inch JBL speaker. Designed in collaboration with Ron Benson, the Benson HR models were originally based on the idea of reproducing Robert's Gibson GA-50 with more power and options. They quickly became the most sought-after studio amps of the era, especially for jazz playing.

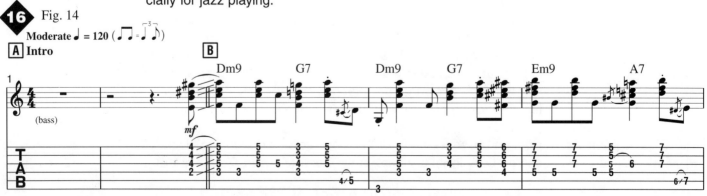

* Tremolo on top two notes only.

Verse

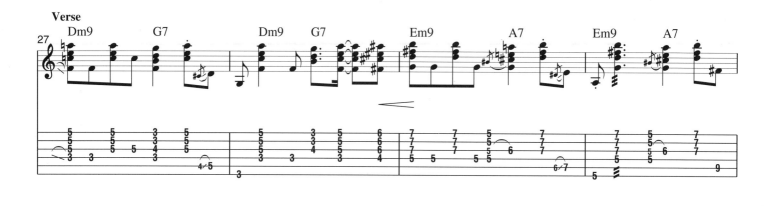

Break
(Band tacet)

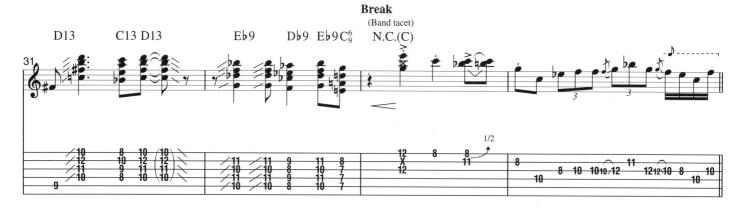

C **Guitar Solo**
(Band in)

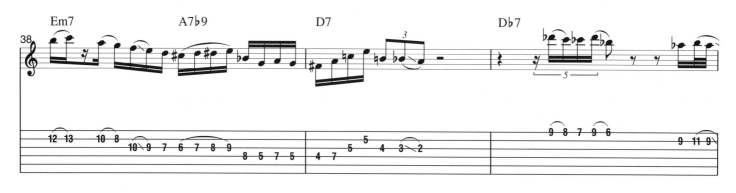

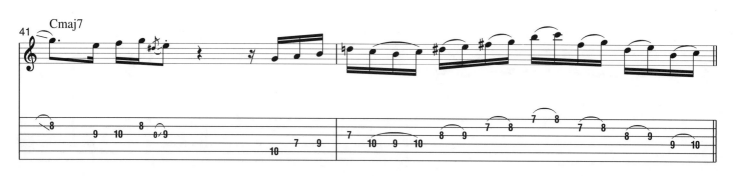

Joe Pass

Fig. 15 — Intro, Head, and Solo

Joe Pass would have come to prominence 10 years earlier had he not been sidelined with drug addiction in the 1950s. Born in New Brunswick, New Jersey, he received guitar lessons, formal and informal, at an early age and began playing professionally when he was 14. Pass was drawn to the East Coast jazz scene and moved to New York City in his twenties. There he developed into a fluent bebop guitarist with a keen harmonic sense, but he also came under the influence of heroin, which cost him many of his best years. Pass entered Synanon in 1960 and ultimately overcame his addiction. His musical career was ignited by the brilliant playing on *Sounds of Synanon* and his Pacific Jazz sessions of the 1960s. By the early 1970s, Pass was one of the leading guitarists in jazz and exhibited a formidable two-prong approach. His command of fretboard harmony and chord-melody style yielded the acclaimed *Virtuoso* albums and resulted in a singular career as a solo performer. Additionally Pass's impressive single-note style marked him as the logical successor to the Charlie Christian-Tal Farlow-Wes Montgomery school of jazz guitar. Both facets are well-documented in a definitive series of recordings spanning over 20 years for Norman Granz's Pablo label.

Joe Pass has been called the "Art Tatum of the guitar" and the "Charlie Parker of the guitar." Hardly glib toss-offs, these allusions refer to his great proficiency with chordal improvisation and horn-like, single-note bebop lines. We are treated to both sides of Pass's artistry in his swinging rendition of "Satin Doll."

Personnel: Trio. Joe Pass, guitar; Ray Brown, bass; Bobby Durham, drums.

Recorded: June 21, 1974, at Fantasy Studios, Berkeley, California.

Arrangement: Pass also plays "Satin Doll" in the standard key of C at a moderate tempo slightly faster than HR. The arrangement is the epitome of swinging straight-ahead jazz, consisting of a brief intro $\boxed{A}$, a statement of the head $\boxed{B}$, and several blowing choruses.

Signatures: Pass plays an unmistakable four-bar intro mixing block chords, single-note passing tones, stride-style voicings of 7th and 10th intervals. His treatment of the head is equally unmistakable. As in Howard Roberts's version, Pass plays the A sections in chords and takes liberties with the bridge, using improvised single-note lines in measures 21–24, and stating the melody in block chords in 25–27. Measure 28 contains a signature turnaround phrase. The solo is replete with Pass signatures, beginning with a swinging bebop break that hints at two familiar jazz melodies: "Joy Spring" in the opening line, and a paraphrase of the "Honeysuckle Rose lick" in measure 37. Other identifiers occur in the bop line of measures 43–44. They contain a favorite ascending motive based on the "Django lick" (see Fig. 14) and a winding sax-like flurry in 16th notes. Another identifier of Pass's bop style is the distinctive neighbor-tone activity and chromaticism in these lines. Similar melodic motion is found in measures 53–57. Blues-oriented swing phrases and groove riffs complement Pass's hard bop playing throughout, as heard in measures 60–61, 82–84, 85–86, and 99–100. Additional attractive contrast is found in Pass's juxtaposition of chord phrases and single-note melodies.

Performance notes: Pass plays the chords in "Satin Doll" with both straight plectrum and *hybrid picking* style. Strumming is confined to block-chord passages and block chords mixed with single notes. Hybrid picking is found in ad lib fills and the partial chords of measures 3–4. Adept at all forms of articulation, Pass primarily used the plectrum for the single-note lines in "Satin Doll."

Sound: Pass's sound is a definitive jazz guitar tone. It was most often produced by an early-1960s Gibson ES-175 with two humbucking pickups. At this point, Pass strung it with medium-gauge D'Aquisto flatwound strings, and plugged into a Polytone 102 combo amp with two eight-inch speakers and one 12-inch speaker.

* Played behind the beat.

YESTERDAYS

Words by Otto Harbach   Music by Jerome Kern

"Yesterdays" is a perennial favorite in the mainstream jazz repertory. Another popular show tune written by composer Jerome Kern, it truly deserves the appellation of standard. The tune is a minor-mode composition with an unusual B section that largely moves through a *cycle of fourths* with altered dominant chords. Both aspects make it an ideal vehicle for elaboration by jazz artists. Though originally composed in a larger form with a different ending, "Yesterdays" is usually played in a jazz context as a repeated 32-bar ABAB structure. The piece inspired three strikingly different arrangements, marking the diverse approaches of Johnny Smith, Tal Farlow, and Wes Montgomery.

Johnny Smith

Fig. 16 — Intro, Head, Solo, and Outro

Few guitarists convey the blend of taste and virtuosity that is Johnny Smith's sonic calling card. His music has an easy, accessible quality which belies its inherent technical demands and sophisticated harmonic aspects—which is one reason "Moonlight in Vermont" was a breakthrough hit record with the general public. Since then he has remained an internationally-acclaimed instrumentalist and one of jazz guitar's most unusual exponents. Johnny Smith was born in Birmingham, Alabama, and is a self-taught player who cites Andres Segovia and Django Rheinhardt as his major influences. He gained his first professional experience with a hillbilly group called the Fenton Brothers. After WWII, Smith joined the N.B.C. staff in New York City where he played trumpet and guitar with various types of combos and orchestras. In the early 1950s he formed a quintet with tenor saxophonist Stan Getz. Their 1952 hit "Moonlight In Vermont" put the Johnny Smith Quintet on the map and resulted in recognition and accolades by the jazz world. From 1953 to 1960, Smith led a number of stellar jazz groups on the East Coast, including the well-knit lineup that produced *Jazz At N.B.C.* and its standout rendition of "Yesterdays."

Smith is renowned for his remarkable prowess on the guitar. He has been called, by his peers, a "scientist" and a perfectionist, because of his fine technique and studied approach. However, his music can also be described as extremely beautiful and moving, as in the case of "Yesterday," which stands as a tribute to Smith's artistry and the clarity of his playing, as well as his arranging abilities and expressiveness.

Personnel: Quintet. Johnny Smith, guitar; Paul Quinchette, saxophone; Sanford Gold, piano; Eddie Safranski, bass; Don Lamond, drums.

Recorded: August, 1953, in New York City.

Arrangement: Smith plays "Yesterdays" in the original key of D minor as a slow ballad with a rubato feel. His arrangement is brief but colorful. It begins with a two-bar solo piano intro. Smith states the 16-bar head [A] in chord-melody style and then comps lightly behind the sax solo. He takes a six-bar guitar solo in single notes at [B], and rejoins the head in chord-melody style for a recap [C] and a final cadence in free time.

Signatures: "Yesterdays" is distinguished by Smith's highly identifiable block-chord style. He plays the melody largely *in clusters*—close-voiced block chords—using a number of altered chords to harmonize the line. This lends a lush impressionistic tinge to the head. The cadence progression in measures 15–16 and in the recap is a prime example of Smith's reharmonization approach. Note the high A maintained as a common tone through the chord changes. Smith's solo is elegant and typical of his understated virtuosity and strong sense of melodic construction. He begins with a brooding minor-mode phrase laced with chromaticism (a paraphrase of "It Ain't Necessarily So") in measures 32–34 and produces a powerful climax with a sweeping sequential run in 16th-note sextuplets in measure 37.

Performance notes: Smith tuned his sixth string down one whole step to D in "Yesterdays." Though prevalent in classical, folk, and blues styles, the practice of *alternate tuning* is not common in jazz—but then, Johnny Smith is an uncommon jazz guitarist. Smith's cluster block chords generally require a far greater stretch than conventional guitar forms. Typically close-voiced, piano-style, these chords are largely comprised of consecutive thirds, or thirds with added seconds. Smith plays these challenging chord forms with remarkable smoothness using a legato approach and maintaining notes to their fullest rhythmic duration. To this end, he often employs shared fingerings to sustain common tones while changing chords, as in measures 2–4, 9–13, and 15–16. Smith was one of the earliest *linear* players in jazz guitar. The position shifting in measure 35 is a superb example of the type of phrase to receive his linear style. The entire tune is delivered with a genuine *rubato rhythm* feel. Endemic to jazz ballad playing, this involves a subtle accelerating and decelerating of the basic time, and an elasticity in the overall rhythm.

Sound: In this period Smith played a custom-made D'Angelico New Yorker archtop acoustic with a scaled-down 16-inch body. It was fitted with a floating Loutone pickup. He most likely plugged it into a unique Ampeg "fountain of sound" amplifier, which he designed, played, and endorsed in the 1950s.

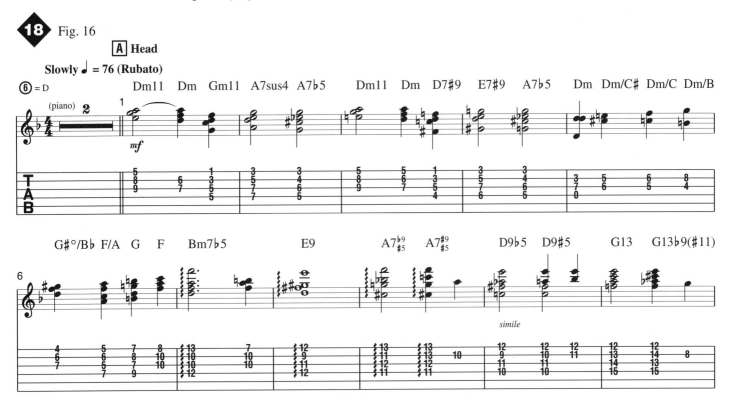

18 Fig. 16

A Head

Slowly ♩ = 76 (Rubato)

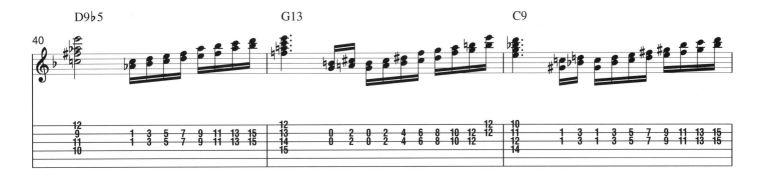

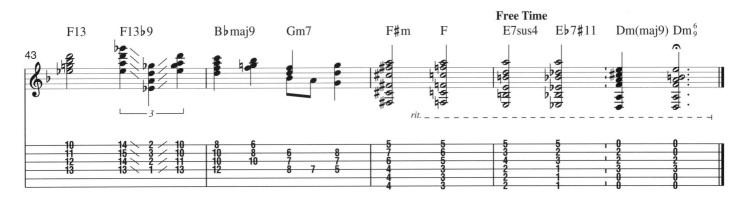

Tal Farlow

Fig. 17 — Head and Solo

Tal Farlow was the reigning proto-bop guitarist of the 1950s. His sound and style bridged the gap between the pioneering guitar work of Charlie Christian in the swing era and the hard bop of Wes Montgomery and Joe Pass to follow. Though speed and physical prowess were hallmarks of his approach, he was graced with a keen harmonic sense and an unerring swing feel. Born and bred in Greensboro, North Carolina, Farlow came to prominence in the extraordinary Red Norvo Trio. While performing at the Haig in Los Angeles with the trio, he was heard by Norman Granz, who signed him for his Verve Records label on the spot. Of the more than thirty albums Farlow recorded in his life, nearly a third were made between 1952 and 1960 for Verve. These are generally considered to be his most innovative artistically and most influential historically. Farlow mastered playing fast tempos with the Norvo Trio. This is what Granz, as producer, preferred from him, and this is what we get in "Yesterdays." A showcase for his fast technique and quick wits, his performance epitomizes the art of up-tempo improvisation and underscores the significance of Farlow's musical impact.

Wes Montgomery said, "Tal came out poppin' and burnin'," and he may as well have been talking about this track. Recorded at the height of his powers in the mid-1950s when Farlow was *the* player on the cutting edge of jazz guitar, "Yesterdays" finds him at his burning best in the favored setting of guitar-piano-bass and is a definitive document of his groundbreaking proto-bop style.

Personnel: Trio. Tal Farlow, guitar; Eddie Costa, piano; Vinnie Burke, bass.

Recorded: June 5, 1956, at Fine Sound, New York City.

Arrangement: Farlow also plays "Yesterdays" in D minor. There the similarities to Smith's version end. Farlow's version receives a blistering up-tempo treatment, which differs substantially from Smith's subtle, chord-melody ballad approach. His arrangement is simpler, and his performance is almost entirely in single notes. The intro 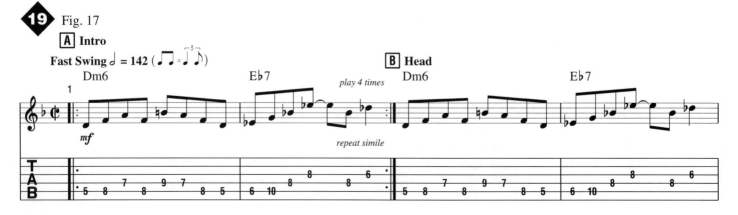A and A sections of the head B (measures 3–6 and 19–23) are dominated by a repetitive figure that becomes the tune's ostinato. Farlow plays a rhythmically animated form of the melody in the B sections. In C – E, he takes three masterful, blowing choruses over the 32-bar form.

Signatures: The virtuosic nature of the guitar playing marks the tune with an unmistakable Farlow brand. In the opening ostinato, he outlines the head vamp (Dm6–E♭7) with quick single-note arpeggios. The repeated-note approach to the melody in measures 7–8 and 23–24 is another identifier of Farlow's style. Though he comes out of the post-Christian swing school, Farlow has a penchant for horn-like bebop vocabulary and phrasing in his solos. This is most evident in the melodic content and rhythmic delivery of long eighth-note streams in measures 41–47, 62–66, 78–82, and 105–112. The chromatic motion of the passage in 91–94 is depictive of Farlow's advanced harmonic sense. He outlines characteristic bop dissonances (A7♯9–A♭7♯9–G7♯9–G♭7♯9) with arpeggios superimposed over the cycle-of-fourths progression. These arpeggios are based on a favorite Farlow 7♯9 motive, which in this solo is also heard in measures 75, 105–106, and 109. Farlow establishes a pattern early in the solo by starting each chorus with a groove riff before proceeding to more ornate passagework in the bulk of the improvisation. This strikes a nice balance between the swing and bebop sides of his musical persona.

Performance notes: Farlow's unique fingering approach and physical dexterity personalize his lines from the opening phrase. The Dm6–E♭7 ostinato figure of the intro and head is a "finger buster," involving five-fret stretches, rapid shifting, seamless bent-knuckle barring, and synchronized alternate and economy picking. Similar wide finger stretches and position shifts typical of "the octopus" abound. The long bop phrase of measures 41-48 is exemplary in its quick shifts and stretches (seven frets in measure 46!) and linear range. In addition to the uncanny fingering changes in his long eighth-note lines, Farlow uses alternate fingerings of the same note—unisons—to produce interesting repeated-note effects in measures 56 and 95–96.

Sound: Farlow's trademark guitar in the mid-1950s was a Gibson ES-350 (nicknamed "the Tal Farlow model") with a Charlie Christian bar pickup in the neck position and a P-90 in the bridge position. He used various 1950s Gibson GA-type combo amps.

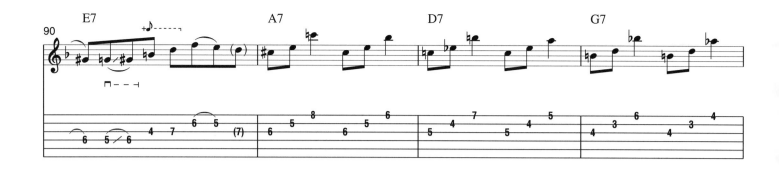

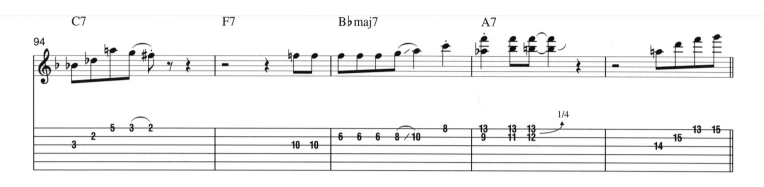

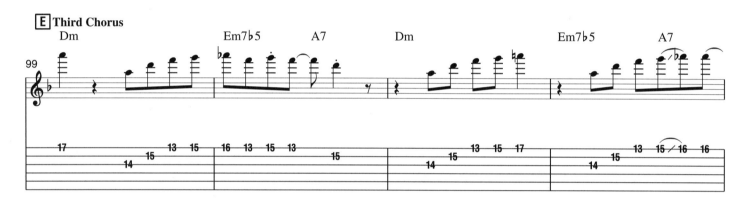

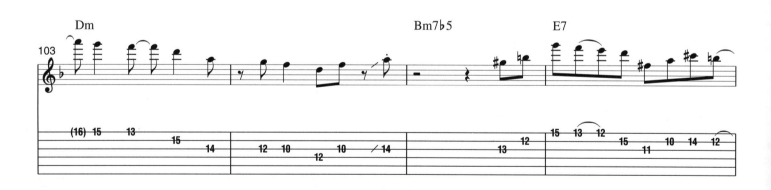

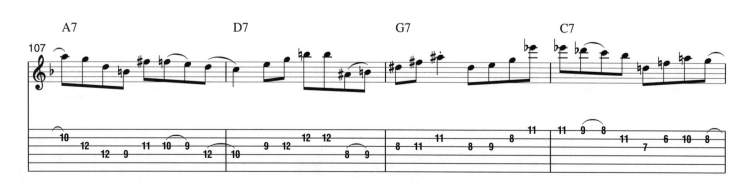

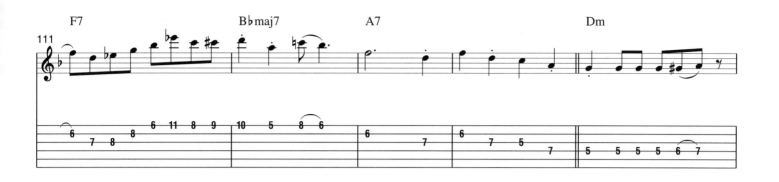

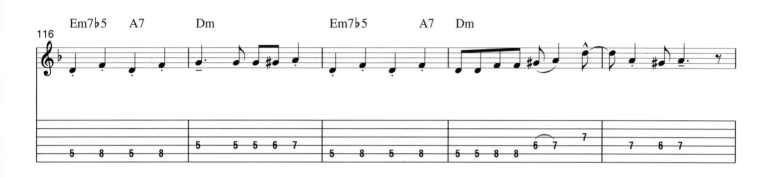

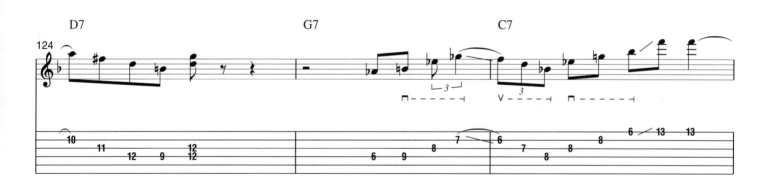

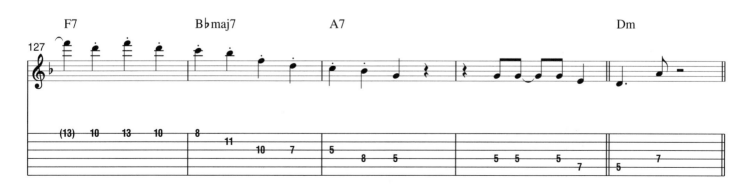

Wes Montgomery

Fig. 18 — Head, Solo, and Outro

Wes Montgomery was the guiding force behind the second major epoch in jazz guitar. If the first belongs to Charlie Christian, then the second belongs to Wes. So profound was his effect on the instrument that to this day, experts define mainstream jazz guitar music as pre-Montgomery or post-Montgomery. Wes Montgomery was born in Indianapolis, Indiana, and picked up the guitar relatively late in life at 19. Brought up in a musical household (brothers Monk and Buddy became noted jazz musicians), he taught himself by diligently copying Charlie Christian solos from records, and by the time he reached his 20th birthday, was gigging regularly at the local 440 Club playing Christian solos. Montgomery's first break came when he secured a job with Lionel Hampton's band in 1948. Grueling road work made up his life for the next two years, and through the experience he became a seasoned jazz player. A devoted family man, Montgomery quit touring in 1950 and stayed in Indianapolis thereafter, playing sporadic club dates while working various non-musical jobs. Montgomery recorded his first album as a leader for Riverside Records, thanks largely to the enthusiastic recommendation of Cannonball Adderley. *The Wes Montgomery Trio* immediately established him as the newest jazz guitar innovator and led to an impressive series of recordings in the 1960s.

The Wes Montgomery Trio featured Montgomery's working trio with Melvin Rhyne and Paul Parker. The organ trio (organ-guitar-drums) remained a favored setting throughout his career, and seemed to bring out his blues and funky jazz influences like no other ensemble. The material was a blend of standards, hard bop numbers, and Montgomery originals. The reinterpreted classic "Yesterdays" was a highlight, and remains an outstanding and definitive Montgomery cut to this day.

Personnel: Trio. Wes Montgomery, guitar; Melvin Rhyne, organ; Paul Parker, drums.

Recorded: October 6, 1959, at Reeves Sound Studios, New York City.

Arrangement: Montgomery also plays "Yesterdays" in D minor. In contrast to Smith's languorous rendering and Farlow's uptempo flight, he performs the tune in an easy-swinging groove—like a minor blues with funk overtones. This is Montgomery's show all the way, and his arrangement is straightforward. He states the melody in the head A takes two solo choruses B and C, recaps the melody D, and goes out on a six-bar tag E.

Signatures: Montgomery's style is heavily blues-based, perhaps more so than any jazz guitarist since Charlie Christian. This strong blues bent is heard in the embellishments of the melody and in solos. Another identifier is the *parallel-octave style* used in the second solo chorus C and in measures 97–116. This became his sonic trademark in years to come. Montgomery's solos typically contain a blend of blues and bebop elements, as is certainly the case in "Yesterdays." His solo is a two-tier structure comprised of single notes in the first 16 measures proceeding to octaves for the remainder of his improvisation. This progression and building up of textures is yet another emblematic facet of his style. Montgomery's soloing always exudes a playful rhythmic feeling guided by a powerful sense of swing, as well as an admirable balance of musical correctness and soulfulness. He redefined the jazz-guitar aesthetic.

Performance notes: Montgomery's most obvious sonic identifier is his use of the thumb to articulate notes, octaves, and chords. This produces a distinctly thick, warm tone, which is often copied but rarely equaled. The thumb stroke in octave playing necessitated a particular technique. Montgomery used fret-hand *muting* to dampen inner strings of the octave shapes. For example, the octave dyads in measure 49 are played on the fifth and third, and fourth and second strings. The muted inner notes are on the fourth and third strings, respectively. The muted strings within his octave shapes actually contribute to the thicker texture of these forms. After Montgomery, these techniques and sounds became staples of jazz guitar. A particularly challenging passage in octaves is found in measures 69–77. Here, the articulation pattern of downstroke-upstroke-downstroke for each triplet is indicated.

Sound: According to producer Orrin Keepnews, Montgomery recorded with borrowed equipment during this session. Kenny Burrell recently confirmed for me that he indeed loaned Wes his L-7 guitar and tweed Fender Deluxe amp for the sessions.

20 Fig. 18

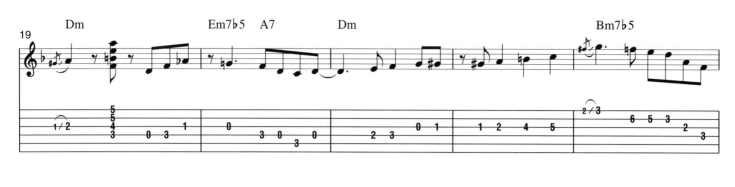

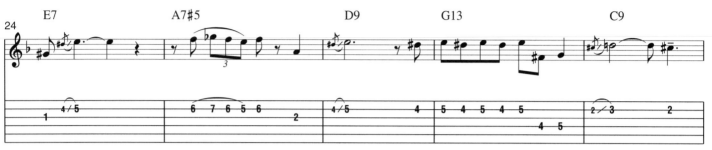

B Guitar Solo: First Chorus

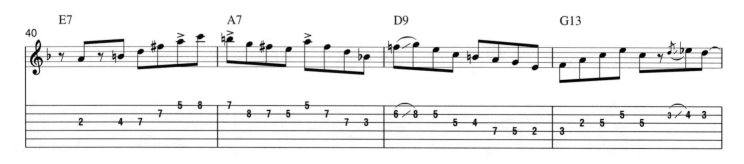

* Octaves include dampened inner string throughout.

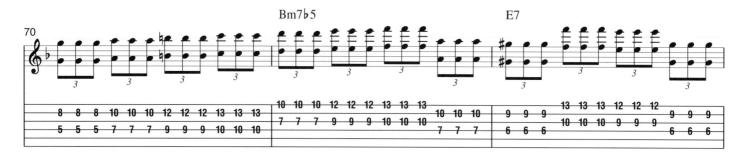
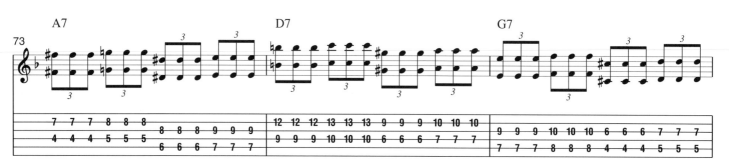
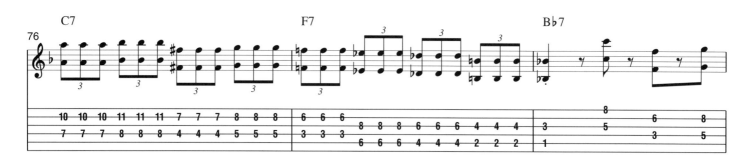
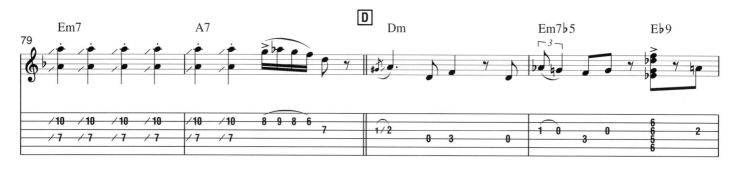

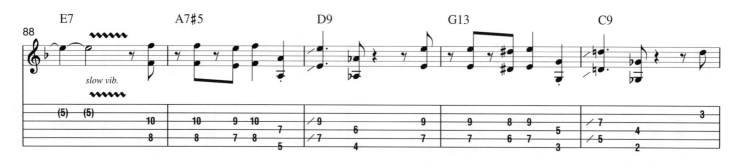

MISTY
Music by Erroll Garner

"Misty" is pianist Erroll Garner's gift to the American musical heritage. It is one of a small handful of precious standards born in the jazz repertory to "cross over" and become a part of modern culture. The fact that it could resonate with pop audiences and jazz aficionados alike, and still does, is a testament to its timeless musical qualities. "Misty" is set in a familiar 32-bar AABA form like countless standards and is graced with an unforgettable melody and one of the prettiest set of changes in the genre. Here, three great guitarists, Barney Kessel, Wes Montgomery, and Howard Roberts, play "Misty" for us with unique and attractively divergent results.

Barney Kessel

Fig. 19 — Head

The Pollwinners (Barney Kessel, Ray Brown, and Shelly Manne) were the toast of the jazz world in the late 1950s. While each was an accomplished instrumentalist with a slew of accolades and a bonafide star in his own right, the combination was sheer musical dynamite and one of the most prodigious guitar-led trios in the history of jazz. This group made several records, all excellent, which highlighted their unique chemistry, redefined the role of the guitar as a focal point of a jazz combo, and raised musical standards in the genre.

Regarded as the successor to the Charlie Christian swing-guitar throne, Barney Kessel also possessed a fluent and adventurous chord style which owed as much to jazz pianists as it did to the guitar masters who preceded him. A case in point is the Pollwinners' rendition of "Misty." It yields an ideal setting for Kessel's thoughtful chord-melody style, undergirded and buoyed by the gentle but supportive rhythm section of Ray Brown and Shelly Manne.

Personnel:	Trio. Barney Kessel, guitar; Ray Brown, bass; Shelly Manne, drums.
Recorded:	August or September, 1960, at Contemporary Records studio, Los Angeles, California.
Arrangement:	Kessel plays "Misty" as a ballad in the unusual key of F major. His arrangement is straightforward. He renders the 32-bar head as a chord-melody statement which never strays appreciably from the melody.
Signatures:	"Misty" is replete with exemplary phrases that illustrate the Kessel chord-melody style. He mixes densities consistently, varying textures from simple dyads (octaves and thirds) and single-note lines, to triads and fuller block chords. A telling phrase occurs in measure 10. Here, he progresses from a two-note contrapuntal passage to a three-note altered chord (F13♭9) and a single-note arpeggio melody. Measure 9 contains a noteworthy *flat-five substitute* reharmonization. Here, Kessel plays Bm11–E7/B on beats 1 and 2 instead of the normally expected Fmaj7 chord. His penchant for harmonizing melodies in parallel thirds is heard in measures 5, 13, 17, 23, 25, and 29. Note the use of grace-note pull-offs to embellish the beginning of the verse refrain in measures 5, 13, and 29. Two particularly attractive and

uncommon turnarounds are found in the head: the first in measure 15 and the second in 31–32. The first is a descending chromatic pattern that alternates between major triads and partial 13th chords. In the second, Kessel plays a series of descending perfect-fourth sonorities for a colorful, impressionistic effect.

Performance notes: Typical of Kessel's chord-melody technique, this reading of "Misty" is played entirely with a pick. All the strummed chords and textures, when not on adjacent strings, are fingered to facilitate fret-hand muting. These fingerings are indicated by Xs in the chord voicings of the staff notation and tablature. A primary facet of the Kessel chord style is his use of *thumb fretting* for bass notes. This technique is found throughout the tune. Definitive examples are found in measures 2 and 4. In measure 2, Kessel plays an F13♭9/C, based on a C diminished shape, which requires an unusual stretch. This chord form may feel awkward, but it is well worth the effort to cultivate.

Sound: Gibson ES-350. (See Fig. 7)

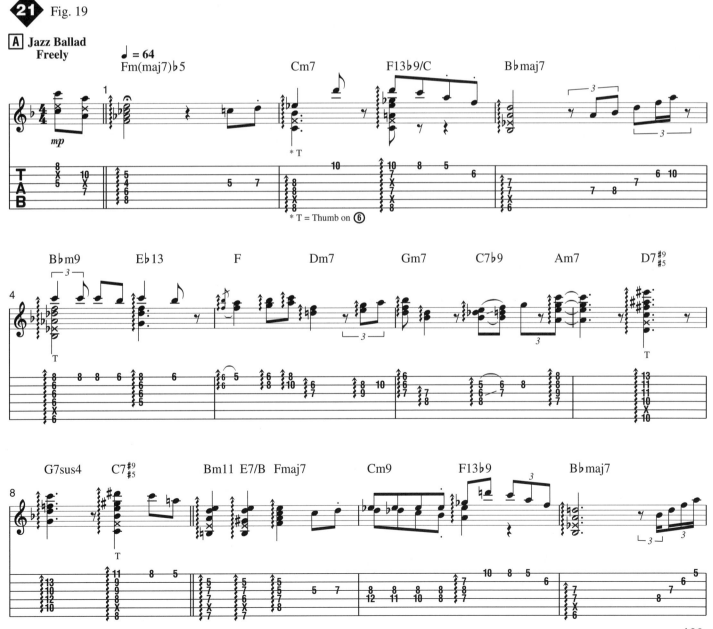

Wes Montgomery

Fig. 20 — Head and Solo

Wes Montgomery's magnificent version of "Misty" was recorded during his Verve years of the mid-1960s. In this phase of his career, he began to make the more commercial recordings that drew a wider audience to his music. Most of these commercial offerings were met with strong critical disapproval among journalists and purists. As if to prove the critics wrong and to reinstate his position as the leading jazz guitarist of the 1960s, Montgomery recorded several live concerts ultimately released on Verve as *Smokin' at the Half Note* and *Willow Weep for Me.* Highly influential to subsequent generations of guitarists, these classic recordings are among the most swinging and definitive jazz performances of his catalog. From this batch, "Misty" stands as one of the finest moments in the repertory.

Recorded at the Half Note in New York City, "Misty" is a balladic masterpiece and another fruitful result of the Wes Montgomery/Wynton Kelly Trio collaboration. It successfully captures the spirit and atmosphere of a top-notch combo performing spontaneous straight-ahead jazz in a roomful of appreciative patrons. Montgomery was the only soloist on this number, and as such, it provides a marvelous showcase for his interpretive and improvisational skills.

Personnel: Quartet. Wes Montgomery, guitar; Wynton Kelly, piano; Paul Chambers, bass; Jimmy Cobb, drums.

Recorded: June 26, 1965, at the Half Note, New York City.

Arrangement: Montgomery also plays "Misty" as a ballad, however in another unusual key: G major. Typical of jazz players reinterpreting ballads, he takes liberties with the song form. Montgomery plays the head [A] in single notes, takes a single-note solo over the complete form in a double-time swing feel [B], solos in octaves over the bridge [C], and returns to the tune in single notes at the original tempo [D]. He closes with an outro [E] that includes a free-time cadenza in   octaves.

Signatures: Montgomery puts his own indelible stamp on "Misty." The head is a decorated rendering of the melody. Here, he adds a number of embellishments in fills and connecting lines between important chord changes and in turnarounds. He also makes some characteristic modifications to the song's time-honored chord changes, as in the bridge, where a substitute set of chords: Em9–A9–Am(maj7)–Am7♭5–A♭13, replaces the more common F♯7–A7–Bm7–E7–Am7–D7 turnaround of most versions. *Motivic development* is pursued at the outset of the solo in the imitative blues riff melodies of measures 34–37. This figure is recalled in measures 54–57. Bebop flurries are found in measures 24–25, 42–44, 72–75, and 119–121. Characteristic ostinato figures are found in measures 63, 70–72, 82–83, and 88–89. Montgomery's patented parallel-octaves are saved for the last bridge and outro.

Performance Notes: Montgomery's fingering of single-note lines has always been a source of consternation among jazz guitar purists. Like many blues and rock guitarists, he never used his pinky, irrespective of the complexity or physical demands of a passage. Montgomery's technique was extremely *linear.* He connected positions laterally up and down the fretboard, and often shifted on a single on a single string. As a result he avoided the normal confines of guitaristic "box playing." Instead his lines overlapped and dovetailed like chord inversions arranged horizontally on the fingerboard. These types of linear phrases occur throughout "Misty." As in all his performances, Montgomery's thumb attack lends a unique round tone to his playing. In "Misty" his thumb articulation adds much to the drama of the outro in measures 128–132 and 138–142. Here, he used a purring tremolo effect with alternating thumb strokes to shade his parallel-octave phrases.

Sound: In this period Montgomery produced his immediately-recognizable tone with various Gibson L-5CES archtop electrics and a solid-state Standel Custom XV amp with one 15-inch speaker. He strung his guitars with heavy-gauge Gibson HiFi flatwound strings.

22 Fig. 20

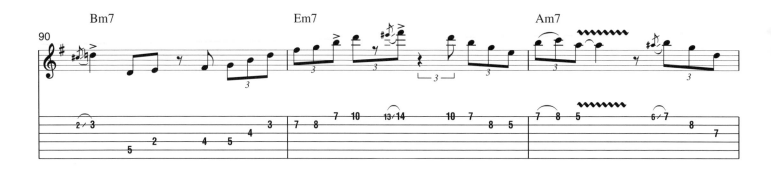

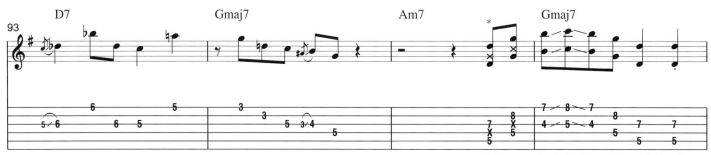

* Octaves are played with dampened inner string throughout.

C Bridge

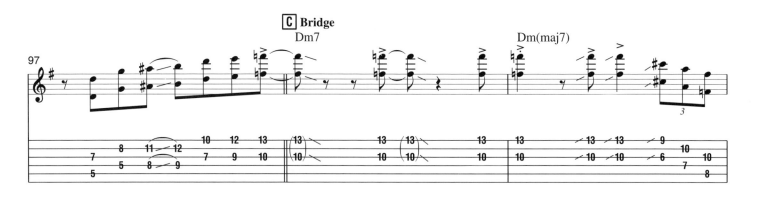

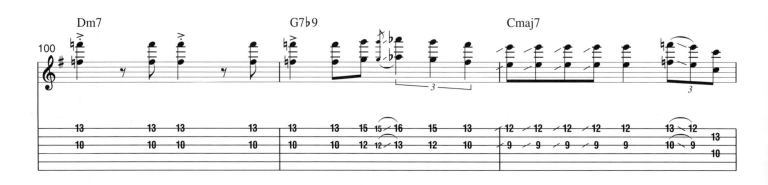

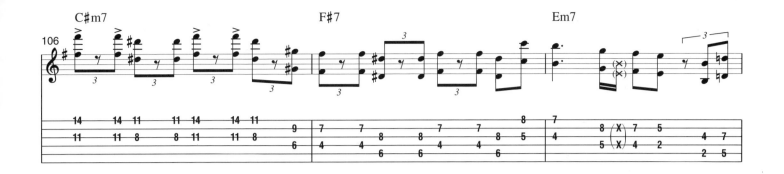

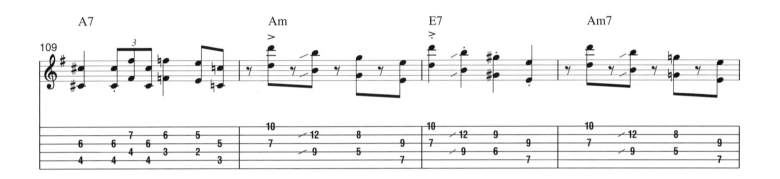

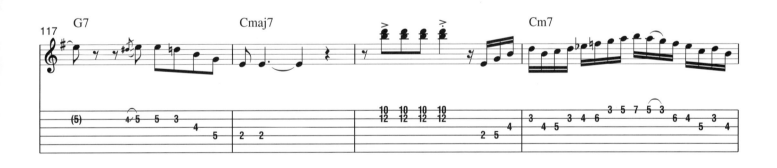

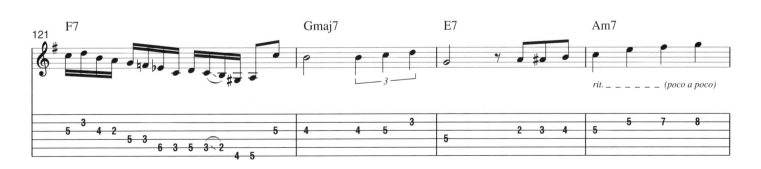

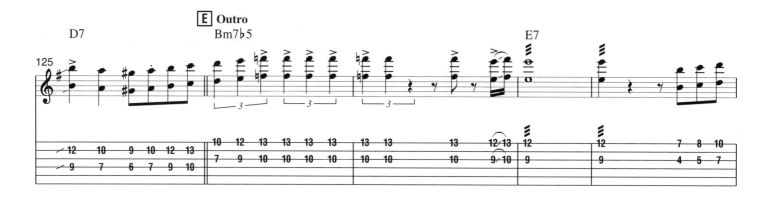

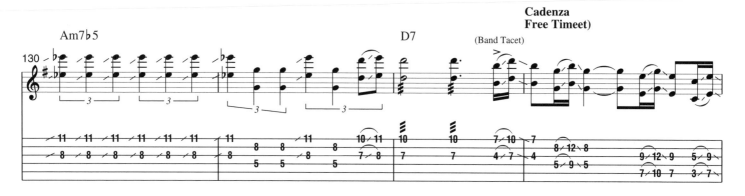

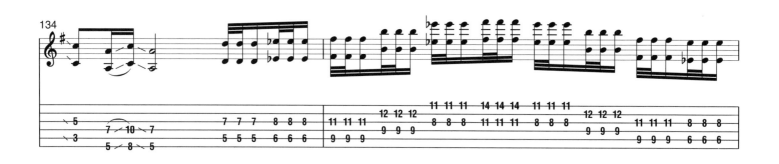

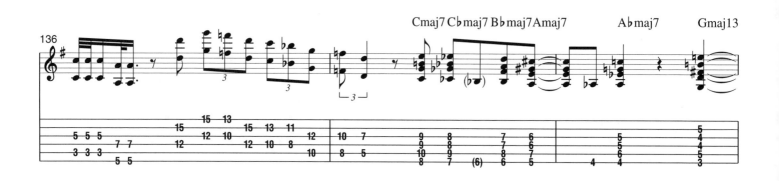

Howard Roberts

Fig. 21 — Intro, Head, Solo, and Outro

A true individualist, Howard Roberts broke new ground in the mid-1960s. During his Capitol Records period, he cultivated a form of jazz in which the average tune length was generally two to three minutes, and improvisations were confined to short partial choruses. Consequently, elaborations of the melody and extemporizing began earlier in the course of an arrangement and solos were usually brief but memorable statements–more accurately, gems. Roberts was not afraid to experiment with conventional formats and liked to bend the rules–often flavoring his arrangements and solos with "fusion" ingredients such as ethnic middle-Eastern runs, impressionistic sonorities, funk rhythms, and overt rock licks. HR's Capitol output was often incorrectly perceived as easy-listening music or blatantly commercial; but make no mistake, he could swing in any context, and everything he touched bore the stamp of a jazzman's interpretation. Such is the case with his unorthodox version of "Misty."

"Misty" received a definitive HR treatment. It is funky, innovative, and unmistakable. His rendition employs the favored ensemble of guitar-organ-bass-drums and distills the trademarks of his uncommon guitar style into a brief but essential whole.

Personnel: Quartet. Howard Roberts, guitar; Henry Cain, organ; Chuck Berghoffer, bass; Larry Bunker, drums.

Recorded: August 13, 1966, at Capitol Records, Hollywood, California.

Arrangement: Roberts plays "Misty" in the standard key of E-flat. His arrangement, however, is anything but standard. In contrast to the Kessel and Montgomery balladic approaches, he treats "Misty" as a medium up-tempo swing number with a strong backbeat feel. Its doubled rhythm values result in a structural change: the standard 32-bar form becomes a 64-bar form. HR's "Misty" is shorter in length and more arranged with the following scheme. A six-bar intro A sets up the head B, where Roberts states the tune's melody with embellishments. The organ takes the bridge melody in C. In D, HR begins his solo instead of completing the form. He improvises over two choruses of the A section. In E, a repeated ii–V–iii–VI progression acts as a coda. The intro figure is recalled as a tag in measures 101–106. HR plays a florid trademark cadenza in measures 107–112.

Signatures: Wes Montgomery once said (*Down Beat:* June 29, 1967) that Roberts's playing had a "nice pattern," and that he could always recognize him by his clean runs, mixed textures and alternation of double-time lines and subtle lines. "Misty" is exemplary, filled with delightfully idiosyncratic HR signatures merging blues and rock licks with bebop and swing lines—all delivered with his unique rhythmic phrasing and dramatic timing. The *pedal-tone* phrase endings in measures 11–12 and 75 are HR identifiers, as is the diminished-scale symmetrical run in measures 77–78. The organ-style double-stop licks in measures 63–64, and the bluesy pull-off riffs in measures 81–82 and 95–96 are other familiar components of his style. Roberts's signature toe-tapping groove riffs are found in measures 54–57, and 84–88. He plays blues-based unison licks in measures 89–91, and funky string bends decorate phrases in measures 15, 36–37, 55–57, and 92. Sweep-picked arpeggios, a staple of the HR style, abound, most notably in measures 13, 26, 60–61, and 69.

Performance notes: Roberts's well-developed technique imparts a gracefulness and smoothness to his playing. Many of his technical concepts are detailed in his fine pedagogical books and instructional columns. HR positioned his picking hand over the neck pickup, and employed a style of picking that he likened to a handwriting posture and the act of drawing of small circles on a piece of paper. This evolved into the nomenclature *circle picking,* which Roberts cited as the most efficient technique for quick single-note playing. It has since become a buzz word in contemporary guitar education. This approach is used for most of his bebop lines and intricate melodies in "Misty."

Sound: HR alternated between an Epiphone Howard Roberts model or his modified black guitar (see Axology) in the mid-1960s. The Epiphone Roberts model was an archtop acoustic-electric designed as an "upgraded ES-175." Its unusual features included an oval soundhole and a floating mini-humbucking pickup fitted at the end of the fingerboard. Roberts strung these with heavy-gauge Gibson Monosteel round-wound strings. At this point, HR most often plugged into a Benson 300HR amp with a 15-inch JBL speaker.

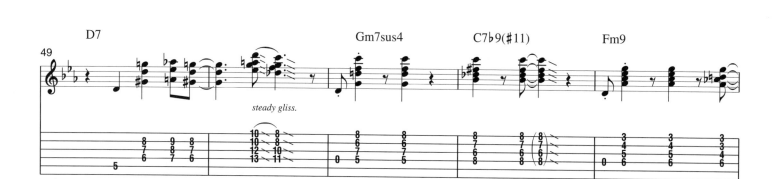

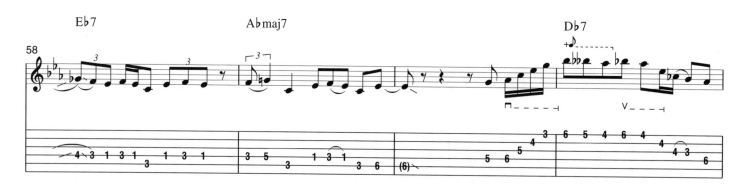

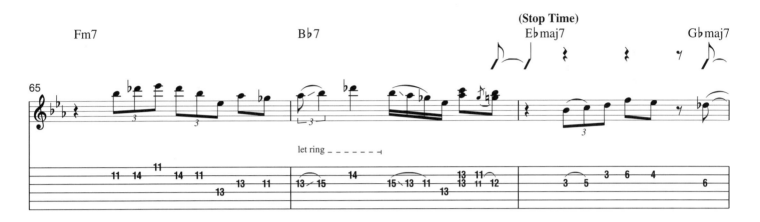

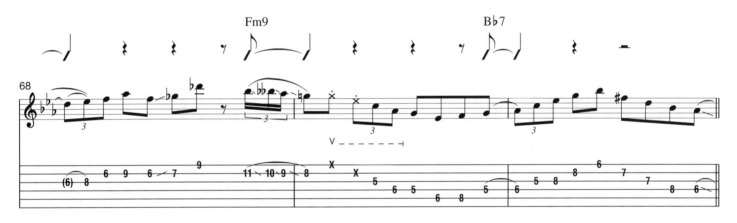

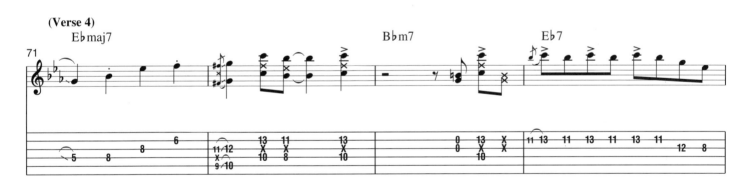

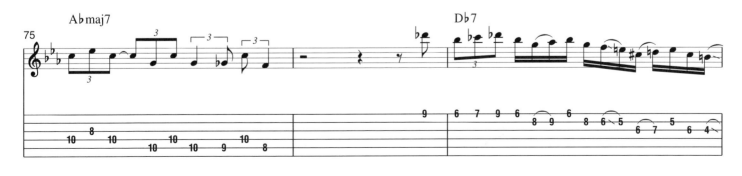

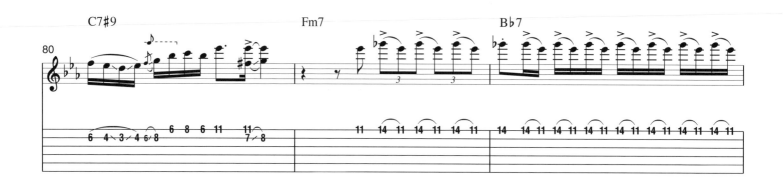

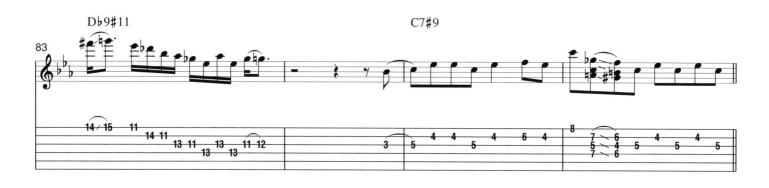

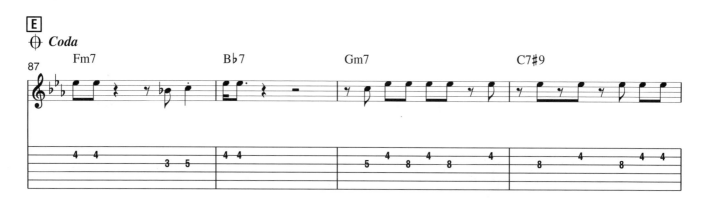

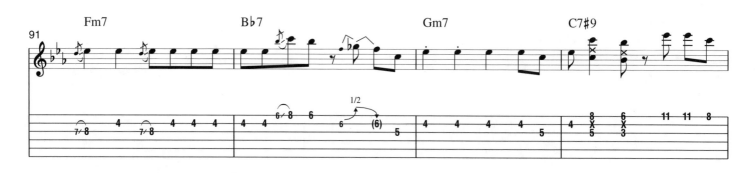

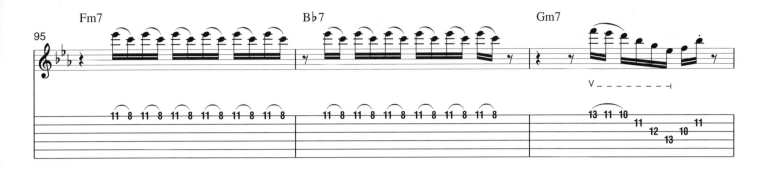

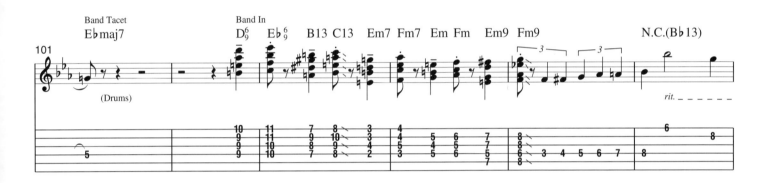

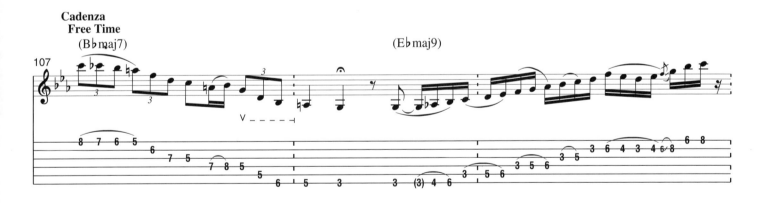

I'LL REMEMBER APRIL

Words and Music by Don Raye, Gene De Paul and Pat Johnson

"I'll Remember April" is another popular standard frequently found in the mainstream jazz repertory. This Raye-De Paul-Johnston evergreen has enjoyed over a half century of exploitation by countless artists, and provided the inspiration for numerous jazz improvisations and compositions—including the harmonic basis of George Russell's famed contrafact "Concerto for Billy the Kid." "I'll Remember April" is set in an unusual 48-bar ABA form: 16 + 16 + 16. Its characteristic fluctuation of major-minor tonal areas in A sections and remote modulations in the bridge have challenged, intrigued and inspired many jazz improvisers to traverse its musical terrain over the years, including guitarists Johnny Smith and Grant Green; each of whom mined new gold from its landscape.

Johnny Smith

Fig. 22 — Intro, Head, and Solo

Johnny Smith was one of the most celebrated jazz guitarists of the early 1950s. The period from 1952-1953 was most auspicious. "Moonlight in Vermont," his collaboration with Stan Getz, had been a serendipitous pop hit, he was a member of the N.B.C. musical staff, and he found favor in the New York jazz community as its most promising new exponent. In 1953 he was in his prime—successfully leading his own groups and recording music regularly for Roost Records. From this phase of his career came the often-lauded *Moods* album and its milestone version of "I'll Remember April."

Smith's rendition of "I'll Remember April" finds him in a setting of two guitars-plus-rhythm section. His take on the classic standard bears his unique imprint; distinguished by a smooth but insistent swing feel and a virtuosic but tasteful handling of the guitar work.

Personnel:	Quartet. Johnny Smith, guitar; Perry Lopez, rhythm guitar; Arnold Fishkin, bass; Don Lamond, drums.
Recorded:	August, 1953, in New York City.
Arrangement:	Smith plays "I'll Remember April" in the standard key of G at a moderately fast tempo. His arrangement begins with an eight-bar intro [A] in half-time feel. The head [B] is played with a swing feel. Smith's solo begins with a two-bar break. He improvises in single notes over one chorus of the form in [C].
Signatures:	The head receives a classic Smith treatment. He plays most of the melody in thirds and close-voiced block chords. The latter are a Smith specialty and identifier. Notable in particular are the clusters in measures 8, 13, 15–17, 27, and 33–34. Another tell-tale Smith identifier is the quick ascending line in measures 44–45. This is a four-octave run consisting of only two notes, G and C, which quickly climbs up the fingerboard to reach C in the highest register. Smith's solo is a one-chorus marvel filled with signature ingredients. His break at measure 51 sets up a *Lydian mode* (G–A–B–C#–D–E–F#) melody, which he exploits in riff form in 53-55. Smith's compositional approach emerges in the sequential imitative phrases of the bridge. The melodious major-pentatonic phrase in measures 85–88 comes across like a fiddle tune adapted to jazz trappings and reveals Smith's Alabama roots. By contrast, his long eighth-note strings in measures 60–66 and

90–97 (he incorporates the "Honeysuckle Rose lick" in measures 91–92) have a pronounced bebop flavor and are strictly uptown. Further contrast is found in the blues-oriented groove riffs in measures 98-100. Such is the diversity of the Smith guitar mosaic.

Performance notes: Smith's block-chord approach is a hallmark of his style. In this up-tempo setting, his precision and dexterity are even more admirable. His seamless chord changing and fluid motion when mixing thirds and clusters is facilitated by a *shared fingering technique.* The technique of sustaining common chord tones generates a legato sound in chord progressions and is a central tenet of his style. Demonstrative examples are found in measures 14–17 and 26–27. Another significant aspect of Smith's technique is his ability to play long linear phrases in a very connected manner. This is a by-product of meticulously-crafted fingering patterns and synchronized accurate picking; the results of which are found in the ascending run in measures 44–45 and the position shifting in 59–66 and 90–97.

Sound: See Fig. 16.

24 Fig. 22

Grant Green

Fig. 23 — Head and Solo

Grant Green is universally acknowledged as the father of funky bebop guitar. His conception effectively reconciles the legacy of horn players like Charlie Parker, Lester Young, and Ike Quebec with rootsy blues and rock 'n' roll. Green was born in St. Louis, Missouri, and was drawn to the guitar in his early teens by the influence of his father and uncle, both of whom were guitarists and played Muddy Waters-style blues in the home. Largely self-taught, his earliest gigs were with a local gospel group, and he subsequently became fluent with boogie-woogie, blues, and rock 'n' roll styles and the standards of the day. In his formative years, Green grew to idolize horn players, especially Charlie Parker, and strove to adapt bop saxophone lines to his vocabulary. By his mid-20s, Green was an accomplished jazz guitarist and sufficiently impressed tenor saxman Lou Donaldson who by chance happened to catch him performing in a St. Louis club. Donaldson, was responsible for Green's record deal with the prestigious Blue Note label and his immersion in the New York City jazz scene. Green's golden years were with Blue Note in the early 1960s. He was not only the house guitarist, recording countless tracks as sideman with the likes of Lee Morgan, Jimmy Smith, Larry Young, and Stanley Turrentine, but a noted and prolific leader with landmark albums like *Idle Moments, Green Street,* and *Grantstand* to his credit. Green was voted Best New Star by *Down Beat* magazine in 1962, and left an extraordinary mainstream jazz catalog with Blue Note before moving into more commercial funk-and-soul territory. That extraordinary catalog is epitomized by tracks like "I'll Remember April."

"I'll Remember April" is a solidly swinging Grant Green excursion. He was at his best as a jazz guitarist in small groups, with the guitar-bass-drums trio proving to be a particularly conducive environment for his spirited invention.

Personnel: Trio. Grant Green, guitar; Wilbur Hare, bass; Al Harewood, drums.

Recorded: August 29, 1961, at Van Gelder Studios, Englewood Cliffs, New Jersey.

Arrangement: Green also plays "I'll Remember April" in the standard key of G. His arrangement of the head A is distinguished by the alternation of a Latin-tinged Afro-Cuban rhythm in measures 1–8 and 33–40, and a straight-ahead swing feel in 9–32 and 41–48. Green begins his solo with a two-bar break and takes three improvised choruses in B, C, and D. His playing consists entirely of single-note lines.

Signatures: Green's mix of bebop lines and funky rhythmic phrases is exemplified in his solo. The former are epitomized by long eighth-note runs in measures 73–79, 113–119, and 180–184, Parker-inspired figures in measures 78, 91, 93–94, 101–103, 139–141, and 155–157, and the bop cadential formulas of measures 80–81, 142–143, and 191–193. The latter are felt in his use of space, staccato punctuation of sparser licks, and overt syncopation. Green employs a favorite motive derived from the "Honeysuckle Rose lick" throughout the solo. Found in varied rhythmic and melodic forms in measures 47–48, 53–54, 56–57, 66–67, 89–90, 93–94, 109–110, 137–138, 153–154, and 185–186, the figure consists of three descending chromatic tones, a downward leap of a 6th, a rising three-note arpeggio, and then stepwise, usually descending, motion. Also noteworthy are the raked and slurred arpeggios in measures 104–108, and the blues-based episode in measures 161–168.

Performance notes: Green favors a laid-back, behind-the-beat phrasing approach, which lends an easy swing feel to his lines. He employs a variety of picking approaches to articulate lines, including alternate picking, economy picking, and consecutive down or up strokes, depending on the intent of the passage. A telling example is found in the raked arpeggios of measures 104–108. There Green uses sweep picking to play the triplet-arpeggio figures to simulate a smeared-glissando sax effect.

Sound: Green played a variety of guitars and amps in the early 1960s. These included a thin hollowbody Gibson ES-330 with P-90 pickups, and two archtop acoustics: a Gibson L-7 and an Epiphone Emperor. The latter were fitted with floating finger-rest pickups. Green strung his guitars with light-gauge, flat-wound strings and used a small heavy pick. He plugged into tweed Fender and Ampeg combo amps.

25 Fig. 23

A Melody

Moderately Fast ♩ = 192
Afro-Cuban

* Chord symbols reflect basic tonality.

134

HOW INSENSITIVE (Insensatez)

Original Words by Vinicius de Moraes
English Words by Norman Gimbel
Music by Antonio Carlos Jobim

Bossa nova was a product of the cross-cultural exchanges of Brazilian and American jazz musicians. The idiom was absorbed into the pop culture via the landmark Getz/Gilberto album and the 1964 Top 10 hit "The Girl from Ipanema." Particularly significant in bossa nova (or "new stream") are the compositions of a leading musical figure, Antonio Carlos Jobim. He is responsible for producing the bulk of the standard repertoire with tunes like "The Girl from Ipanema," "One Note Samba," "Desafinado," "Wave," "Corcovado," and "How Insensitive." "How Insensitive" is a frequently-recorded bossa nova standard, especially poignant with its minor modality and unusual two-part 32-bar form. Bossa nova music is guitar music—which is unusual as jazz is typically defined by wind and keyboard instruments—and has always been dependent on the guitar as a generator of harmony and its primary rhythm instrument. How this figures in two distinctly different guitar-based treatments of "How Insensitive" makes for an engrossing look at the artistry of Pat Martino and Emily Remler.

Pat Martino

Fig. 24 — Intro, Head, and Solo

Pat Martino is one of the most important jazz guitarists of the modern era. Respected in all sectors (Jerry Garcia and Peter Townshend are among his fans), he is a true musical globalist capable of expressiveness and innovation in any genre, and is a master of the high art of bebop improvisation. Born in Philadelphia, PA, Martino was exposed to jazz and the guitar by his father. He was drawn to the styles of Johnny Smith and Wes Montgomery as well as John Coltrane, Art Farmer, and Art Blakey's Jazz Messengers. Something of a prodigy, Martino is self-taught on the guitar and mastered the fundamentals before his teen years. The road was his school. He turned pro at fifteen and began touring with Willis Jackson, Lloyd Price, and numerous R&B acts on the chitlin' circuit. Martino served his jazz apprenticeship in organ-led groups as sideman for Jimmy Smith, Jack McDuff, Don Patterson, Groove Holmes, and others. By the time he was 21, he was a fixture of the New York City hard bop community and began an ambitious series of albums as leader for Prestige Records. Martino continued his musical odyssey in the 1970s and to the present on such offerings as *The Visit, Consciousness, Live!, Joyous Lake, The Maker,* and *All Sides Now.* Martino covered "How Insensitive" in 1972 on *The Visit* (currently issued as *Footprints*). This was his first date as a leader after the Prestige years. Comprised of standards and straight-ahead jazz, it can be seen as a return to the roots after experimentation with ethnic sounds, fusion, and mathematical music in the 1960s.

"How Insensitive" embodies the joyous and near-telepathic musical rapport of soloist Pat Martino and accompanist Bobby Rose. Rose, an accomplished guitarist from their native Philadelphia, has been Martino's regular partner since the 1960s. The Martino/Rose interaction transforms the sultry bossa nova tune into a jazz guitar duet augmented by a rhythm section. The song was a natural choice. Its darker brooding tonal center is particularly conducive to Martino's minor-based improvisational tendencies, and its slower tempo serves as an ideal springboard for his spellbinding florid passagework.

Personnel:	Quartet. Pat Martino, guitar; Bobby Rose, rhythm guitar; Richard Davis, bass; Billy Higgins, drums.

Recorded: March 24, 1972, at the RCA Building in New York City, NY.

Arrangement: Martino plays "How Insensitive" in the original key of D minor. His is a straight-forward arrangement. A four-bar intro [A] establishes the tune's harmonic foundation. Martino plays the 32-bar head twice, first in single notes in [B], and then in octaves [C]. He takes two improvised choruses over the form in [D] and [E].

Signatures: The Martino approach and sound are recognizable from the opening notes. Martino is a hard bop musician in the tradition of John Coltrane and similarly favors a well-articulated approach to single-note playing dominated by 16th notes rather than eighth notes. This is particularly true in slow or medium tempo tunes. The single-note playing in the fills of [B] and the solo choruses are strong identifiers of Martino's style. These unmistakable lines are performed as long streams of rapid 16th notes which, in relation to the song's pulse, produce a *double-timing* of the rhythm. Many have further identified Martino by his unique sense of time and the rhythmic placement of his lines. In measures 106–108, 116–117, and 125–129, he exploits a trademark device of placing repeated patterns in three 16th-note groups. This results in a *three-against-four hemiola* effect. The florid style of his double-timed lines is nicely contrasted by riff-like ostinato figures in measures 69–71 (note the shifted rhythm in this phrase), 91–92, 101–103, 106–111, and 125–129. The latter is a clear allusion to Wes Montgomery, as it was one of his favorite riff melodies.

Performance notes: Pat recently disclosed an interesting performance point regarding "How Insensitive." He uses the round end of the pick when playing octaves, as in [C]. This produces a distinctive timbre with more mass, and can impart a rich quality to octaves similar to Wes Montgomery's thumb attack. Martino also applies this technique to single-note lines in ballads.

Sound: In the 1970s, Pat used a custom-built Sam Koontz archtop electric. This unique instrument had a single Florentine cutaway shape, a floating pickup, and an oval soundhole. He strung the guitar with heavy-gauge round-wound strings (.013–.056), set it up with high action, and employed an ultra-heavy stone pick. Bobby Rose played a late-1960s Gibson L-5 with medium-gauge strings (.012–.052) and used finger-plucking for a softer pianistic effect. For the session both guitarists plugged into Fender Twin Reverb amps.

 Fig. 24

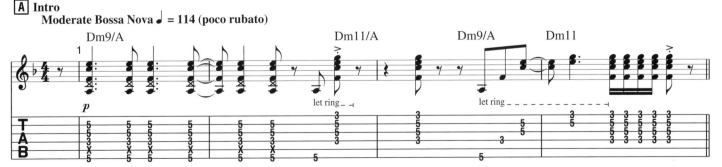

*All octaves played with deadened middle stg.

Emily Remler

Fig. 25 — Solo

While certainly a great *female* guitarist, Emily Remler will always be remembered as a great guitarist, period. Her musicianship and chops put her squarely in the category of artistry without qualification. Born in New York City, NY, Remler grew up listening to the rock, folk, and pop sounds of the day. While attending Boston's Berklee School of Music, jazz caught her ear and she turned her interest and her energies to the music of Charlie Christian, Paul Desmond, and Wes Montgomery. Upon graduating Berklee, Remler relocated to New Orleans, where she soon became one of the busiest guitarists in town. There, a fortuitous meeting with Herb Ellis led to her appearance at the 1978 Concord Jazz Festival and a subsequent contract with Concord Records. Remler produced an impressive series of albums in the 1980s, with music ranging from straight-ahead blowing jazz and hard bop to ballads and elegant guitar duets. She died in 1990 leaving a solid recorded legacy exemplified by tracks like "How Insensitive."

Emily Remler casts "How Insensitive" as a duet with guitarist Larry Coryell. Their guitar-intensive version captures the lilting rhythms of Brazilian music and grafts them onto the bebop branch of the American jazz tree. This excerpt presents Remler's superb three-chorus guitar solo.

Personnel:	Duet. Emily Remler and Larry Coryell, guitars.
Recorded:	August, 1985, at Coast Recorders, San Francisco, California.
Arrangement:	Remler also plays "How Insensitive" in the original key of D minor. She takes three solo choruses over the form in $\boxed{A}$, $\boxed{B}$, and $\boxed{C}$, following Coryell's opening solo.
Signatures:	Remler's solo contains a mixture of the old and the new—mainstream lines blended with a smattering of blues-rock tangents. Her statement builds in complexity, activity, and drama. Remler speaks the bebop language fluently and includes numerous references to her influences, particularly Wes Montgomery and Pat Martino. The sequential legato figure in measure 28, and rising augmented arpeggios in measures 24 and 77 are familiar Montgomery motives. The double-timed flurries in measures 45–47 and 79–80, the pentatonic ostinatos of measures 53–57, and the chromaticized pattern of slurred triads in measures 81–82 are reminiscent of Martino's style and phrasing. Remler employs *thematic development* throughout. She plays three-note figures as a rolling ostinato phrase in measures 36–43. These rhythmically-charged figures are adjusted to suit the changing harmony and are expanded intervallically in measures 42 and 43. Similar development of repeated patterns occurs in measures 17–21, 49–52, and 85–91. In measures 65–70, she subjects double stops to this procedure. Perhaps a vestige of her early rock influences, Remler's vibrato is more modern and pronounced than most traditional bebop guitarists.
Performance notes:	A chordal ensemble intro begins the solo in measures 1–6. Here, Remler plucks the chords rhythmically with her fingers for a strong Brazilian chord-melody result. Her single-note lines beginning in measure 8 are played with a pick. Remler employs articulation and fingerings indigenous to the modern bebop guitar style for most of her solo.

Sound: Luthier Boger Borys believes that this may be one of the earliest tracks to feature Remler's Borys guitar. Made in 1985, this was a BG-100 archtop electric with a 16-inch laminated body. It was fitted with two built-in Guild humbuckers. Remler generally strung her guitars with D'Addario medium-light gauge strings, beginning with an .011 on the high E. She used a Fender extra-heavy 1.21mm pick. Her amplifier of choice was a Polytone or a Fender Twin Reverb.

27 Fig. 25

A **First Chorus**

Moderate Bossa Nova ♩ = 114 **Rubato Tempo**

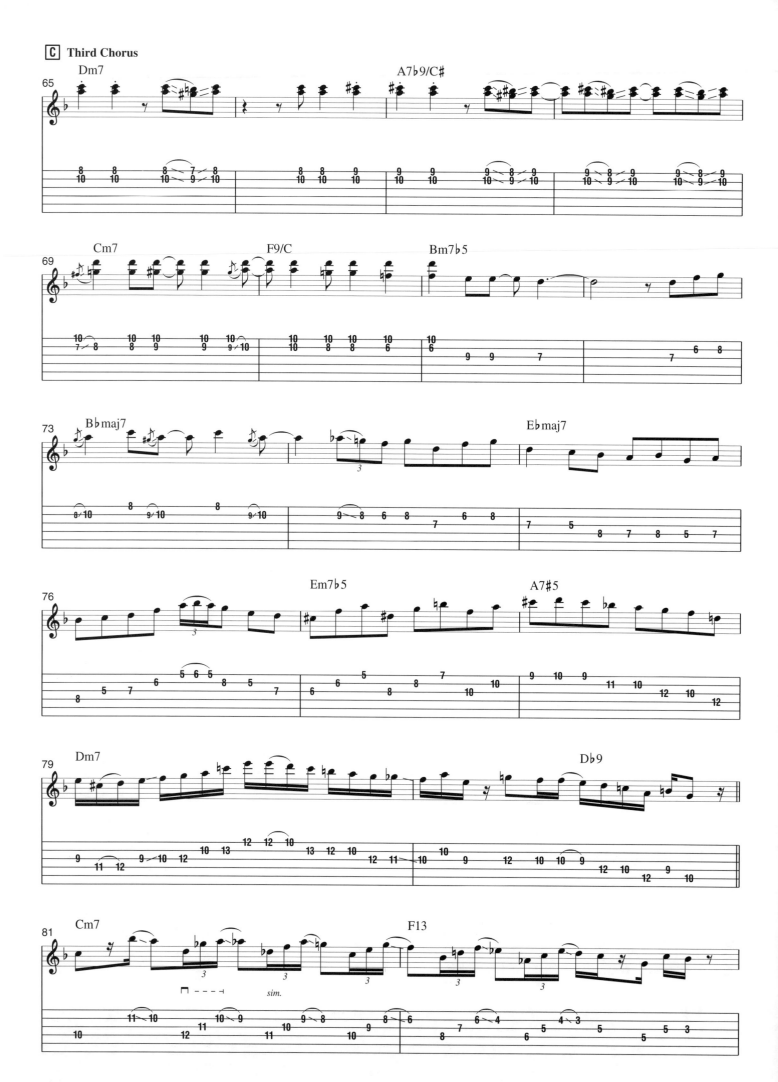

Guitar Notation Legend

Guitar Music can be notated three different ways: on a *musical staff*, in *tablature*, and in *rhythm slashes*.

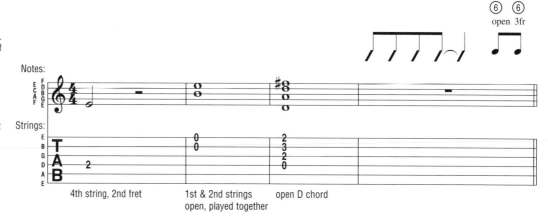

RHYTHM SLASHES are written above the staff. Strum chords in the rhythm indicated. Use the chord diagrams found at the top of the first page of the transcription for the appropriate chord voicings. Round noteheads indicate single notes.

THE MUSICAL STAFF shows pitches and rhythms and is divided by bar lines into measures. Pitches are named after the first seven letters of the alphabet.

TABLATURE graphically represents the guitar fingerboard. Each horizontal line represents a a string, and each number represents a fret.

Definitions for Special Guitar Notation

HALF-STEP BEND: Strike the note and bend up 1/2 step.

BEND AND RELEASE: Strike the note and bend up as indicated, then release back to the original note. Only the first note is struck.

VIBRATO: The string is vibrated by rapidly bending and releasing the note with the fretting hand.

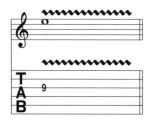

LEGATO SLIDE: Strike the first note and then slide the same fret-hand finger up or down to the second note. The second note is not struck.

WHOLE-STEP BEND: Strike the note and bend up one step.

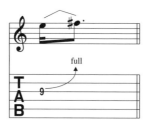

PRE-BEND: Bend the note as indicated, then strike it.

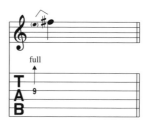

WIDE VIBRATO: The pitch is varied to a greater degree by vibrating with the fretting hand.

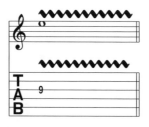

SHIFT SLIDE: Same as legato slide, except the second note is struck.

GRACE NOTE BEND: Strike the note and bend up as indicated. The first note does not take up any time.

PRE-BEND AND RELEASE: Bend the note as indicated. Strike it and release the bend back to the original note.

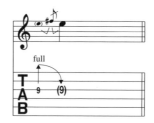

HAMMER-ON: Strike the first (lower) note with one finger, then sound the higher note (on the same string) with another finger by fretting it without picking.

TRILL: Very rapidly alternate between the notes indicated by continuously hammering on and pulling off.

SLIGHT (MICROTONE) BEND: Strike the note and bend up 1/4 step.

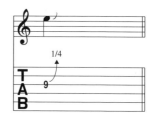

UNISON BEND: Strike the two notes simultaneously and bend the lower note up to the pitch of the higher.

PULL-OFF: Place both fingers on the notes to be sounded. Strike the first note and without picking, pull the finger off to sound the second (lower) note.

TAPPING: Hammer ("tap") the fret indicated with the pick-hand index or middle finger and pull off to the note fretted by the fret hand.

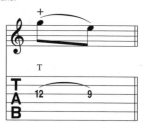

158

NATURAL HARMONIC: Strike the note while the fret-hand lightly touches the string directly over the fret indicated.

PINCH HARMONIC: The note is fretted normally and a harmonic is produced by adding the edge of the thumb or the tip of the index finger of the pick hand to the normal pick attack.

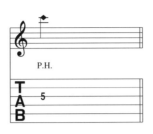

HARP HARMONIC: The note is fretted normally and a harmonic is produced by gently resting the pick hand's index finger directly above the indicated fret (in parentheses) while the pick hand's thumb or pick assists by plucking the appropriate string.

PICK SCRAPE: The edge of the pick is rubbed down (or up) the string, producing a scratchy sound.

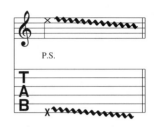

MUFFLED STRINGS: A percussive sound is produced by laying the fret hand across the string(s) without depressing, and striking them with the pick hand.

PALM MUTING: The note is partially muted by the pick hand lightly touching the string(s) just before the bridge.

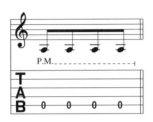

RAKE: Drag the pick across the strings indicated with a single motion.

TREMOLO PICKING: The note is picked as rapidly and continuously as possible.

ARPEGGIATE: Play the notes of the chord indicated by quickly rolling them from bottom to top.

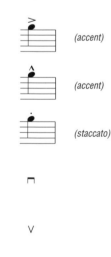

VIBRATO BAR DIVE AND RETURN: The pitch of the note or chord is dropped a specified number of steps (in rhythm) then returned to the original pitch.

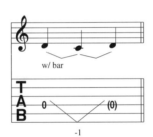

VIBRATO BAR SCOOP: Depress the bar just before striking the note, then quickly release the bar.

VIBRATO BAR DIP: Strike the note and then immediately drop a specified number of steps, then release back to the original pitch.

Additional Musical Definitions

(accent)	• Accentuate note (play it louder)	
(accent)	• Accentuate note with great intensity	
(staccato)	• Play the note short	
	• Downstroke	
	• Upstroke	
D.S. al Coda	• Go back to the sign (𝄋), then play until the measure marked "**To Coda**," then skip to the section labelled "**Coda**."	
D.S. al Fine	• Go back to the beginning of the song and play until the measure marked "**Fine**" (end).	

Rhy. Fig.	• Label used to recall a recurring accompaniment pattern (usually chordal).
Riff	• Label used to recall composed, melodic lines (usually single notes) which recur.
Fill	• Label used to identify a brief melodic figure which is to be inserted into the arrangement.
Rhy. Fill	• A chordal version of a Fill.
tacet	• Instrument is silent (drops out).

• Repeat measures between signs.

1. 2.

• When a repeated section has different endings, play the first ending only the first time and the second ending only the second time.

NOTE: Tablature numbers in parentheses mean:
1. The note is being sustained over a system (note in standard notation is tied), or
2. The note is sustained, but a new articulation (such as a hammer-on, pull-off, slide or vibrato begins, or
3. The note is a barely audible "ghost" note (note in standard notation is also in parentheses).